MW00907926

Many thanks to a friend and mentor,
Duncan Nanney, a Pisces,
as well as companions along the way:

ARIES
Meera Lester

TAURUS
Michael Hammond, Lindy Schasiepen, John Skonberg

GEMINI
Christine Finnan, C.J. Marrow, Sally Sloan

CANCER
Guy Griffiths, Wolfgang and Waultraud Heinritz

LEO
Ann Shotland

VIRGO
Jean Hammond, Vincent Hillyer, Carl Horvitz,
Janice Tomlinson

LIBRA
Dick Hammond, Bob May, Bud Morgan,
Alexandra Hammond

SCORPIO
Phyllis Butler, Sharon Munz

SAGITTARIUS
Dotte Crowder, John Wilson

CAPRICORN
Vern Appleby, Barbara Bladen

AQUARIUS
Clare Trusel

PISCES
Christina Skonberg

♈ *ARIES*

♉ *TAURUS*

♊ *GEMINI*

♋ *CANCER*

♌ *LEO*

♍ *VIRGO*

♎ *LIBRA*

♏ *SCORPIO*

♐ *SAGITTARIUS*

♑ *CAPRICORN*

♒ *AQUARIUS*

♓ *PISCES*

CONTENTS

fire sign

earth sign

air sign

water sign

INTRODUCTION

Four thousand years ago a high priestess of the goddess Astarte turned her face to the stars that blazed and glittered in a midnight sky. What she discerned might have launched an army on the path of conquest or defeat. More recently, the wisdom of the stars was sought on behalf of the President of the United States.

Whether science fact or science fiction, everyone has at least a passing curiosity about astrology. Rare is the person who doesn't know his or her own sign and doesn't feel an affinity toward those who share it.

To plan a party around one's sign or the sign of a lover is to celebrate the very essence of self. To share this occasion with others born under the same sign is to invite a kind of cosmic communion.

Every sign is special, every sign unique, just as completely individual as the parties that each inspires.

One would never serve a delicate, discriminating Virgo the same hot and hearty cassoulet that delights a restless, roving Sagittarian. Though all Virgos are far from virgins—some are congenital heart breakers—there's nothing casual about their approach to food. It's just as unlikely that home loving Cancerians, the Jewish mamas—or papas!—of the cosmos, would ever be content with the poetic party fare of a Pisces.

Given the continuing popularity of astrologers, astrology columns, classes and books, this cookbook has been written adapting the intriguing distinctions of the zodiac to party planning.

Isn't a birthday everybody's favorite occasion for a get together and isn't the sign of the celebrant a natural theme and conversation piece?

HEAVENLY PARTIES features twelve entirely different parties with complete menus and recipes tailored to each astrological sign. They range in size and scope from a romantic dinner for two in keeping with the amorous whims of Libra, the astro love child, to the ultimate in elegance worthy of super cool Capricorn—a cocktail party in the Cary Grant tradition; and include everything from a seance for witchy Scorpio to an Aquarian progressive dinner.

We've pulled out all the stops, believing that on one night at least it's okay to forget about those big bad Cs (calories, cholesterol, and cost). The parties are lavish—some of us believe our birthdays should be national holidays! Each has been carefully organized so that last minute chores are kept to an absolute minimum. Our party plan virtually guarantees that whatever your sign—you'll be the star.

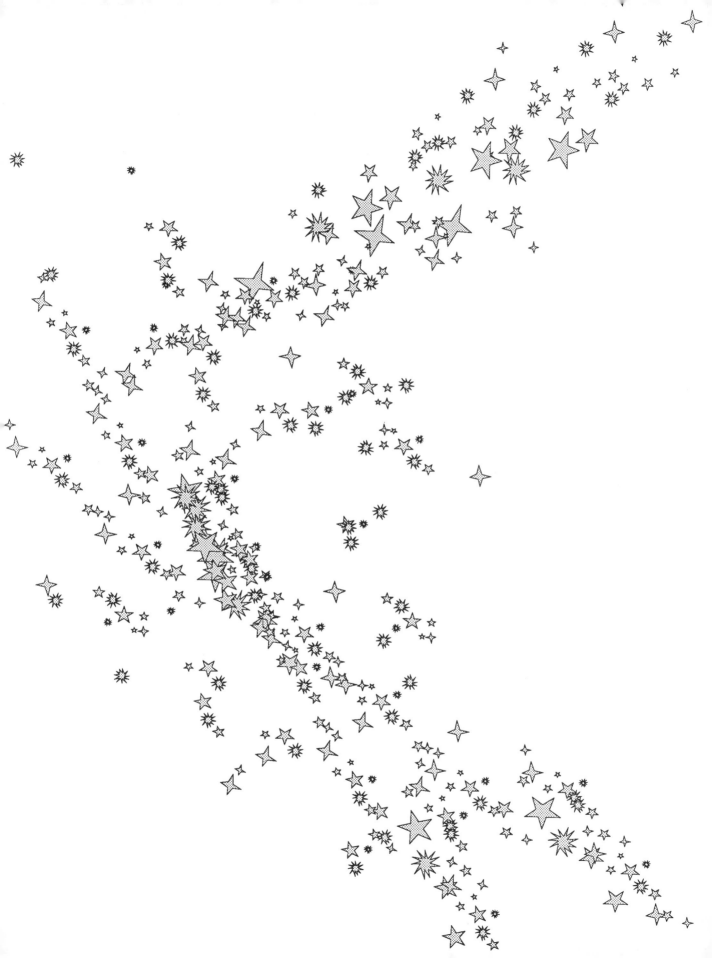

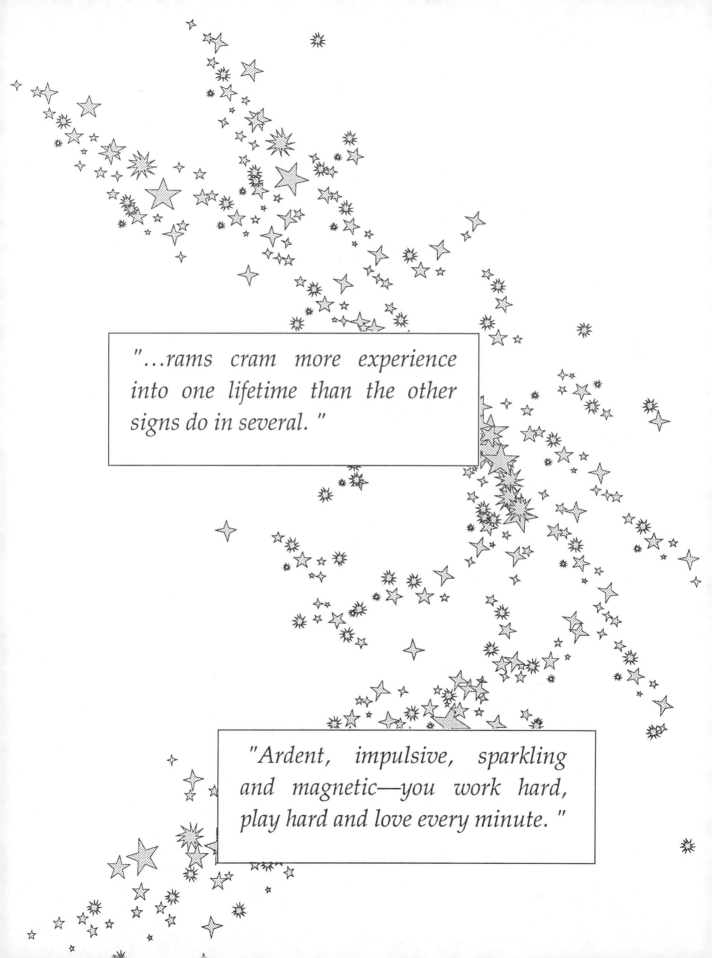

"...rams cram more experience into one lifetime than the other signs do in several. "

"Ardent, impulsive, sparkling and magnetic—you work hard, play hard and love every minute. "

ARIES
Spring Brunch for 20

Mimosas

Skewers of Bacon, Chicken Liver, Sausage, Mushrooms,
Water Chestnuts, Tomatoes, Peppers, Onions

Cheese and Chili Squares

Croissants with Crème Suisse – Sweet Butter
– Preserves

Grapefruit Salad with Mint Lime Dressing

Mocha Mousse
Espresso and Cappucino

ARIES

March 21-April 19

Confidentially, there's nobody I'd rather start the day with than Aries. Ummmm, just to think of all that Mars energy!

As the first sign in the astrological chart, the "baby" of the cosmos, Aries is always young—always ready for change and challenge. Pushy, you say? Of course! Aries wasn't nicknamed the ram for nothing. Yet who can resist an occasional display of fireworks?

Never bashful about voicing their opinions, Aries will talk back to a traffic cop or a gangster with equal candor.

As the first astrological sign, Aries represents birth; and, like any infant, the cosmic kid has a "me first" attitude that can *appear* selfish. But consider…is he/she really? A baby is so adorably appreciative—all smiles, coos and caresses for those who answer distress calls.

Does a baby ever stop to ponder where the next bottle or fresh diaper is coming from? Of course not! And who could resist such disarming innocence and optimism?

Perhaps it's that delightful naiveté that explains the famous Aries fearlessness. The toddler tumbles but invariably struggles up again ready for another go at queen/king of the mountain. Mind you, it isn't just for the glory. This sign must have change and challenge to survive.

What would you Arians ever do if the world reached a state of Utopia?

What would that classic Arian, Scarlett O'Hara have done if she'd actually snared Ashley or discovered sooner that Rhett was the one who really rang her chimes?

Of course no Aries woman believes for an instant that Scarlett wouldn't get Rhett back. But an Aries male is always quick to counter, "Yes, but it would have to be on Rhett's terms." Well, who knows. After all ... tomorrow is another day.

Nobody, but nobody loves a challenge more than you do, Ari. If for no other reason than that you rams cram more experience into one lifetime than the other signs do in several. You've got so many irons in the fire that it sounds like the Anvil Chorus around your place. The ensuing sparks liven up the world.

Action and independence are essentials to you but so is romance. You simply must have love in your life for the ultimate adventure. It's true, you exhaust your lovers and other friends but never, never bore them. That Super Person stance of yours may scare off a few wimps but then when have you ever cared for creampuffs?

Yes, of course, you're pushy. Everybody knows that! Ardent, impulsive, sparkling and magnetic—you work hard, play hard and love every minute. Who can resist that combination?

No one, Ari—at least no one *you'd* care to know.

fire sign

Celebrating the Rites of Spring with Aries —
A Brunch for 20

Action, reaction—you adore every second. Visionary Aries thrives on excitement and intrigue—just think of astro siblings, Jerry Brown and Gloria Steinem. Naturally that means people and parties! Robin Hood, an archetypical Aries, had his Merry Men, didn't he? —plus Maid Marian to inspire rescues and revels.

Like most knights, you adore pomp and pageantry, but run a little short on practicality. You'd about as soon conquer a new castle as change a lightbulb in the old one.

Not for you the pride of the carefully polished tea service that casts a special glow on classy Capricorn, the endless hours of taste piloting that results in subtle Virgo's Absolutely Perfect Souffle, or the sweet nothings murmured by poetic Pisces while carefully coaxing a simple bouquet into a floral extravaganza.

The trail blazer of the cosmos, you're best off leaving someone else to build the settlement. Admittedly, your attention span is limited. What you wanted yesterday can look a bit ho-hum today. Tomorrow? The world, of course, followed next week by the galaxy.

In the meantime, a spring brunch carefully stage managed to allow you to hold court throughout is a natural. Plan tingly, tangy, spicy dishes that underscore those same qualities in yourself.

Life with an Aries is a plunge into adventure. Just think of the fire of Rachmanioff, the brilliance of Van Gough, the courage of Houdini. All that verve and vitality belong in the menu as well. Naturally guests will include the movers and shakers of the ram's private preserve. Would an Aries settle for anything else? Brunches are tailor made for such 200-watt personalities who must often eat and run.

For background music, look to Aries greats such as Bach, Pearl Bailey,

Toscanini, Diana Ross or Leopold Stokowski, though you could favor the lurking Lancelot within with a mad, merry madrigal or two.

Easy to plan, easy to prepare, but loaded with your special sizzle and sass, the menu reflects your own sense of fun and originality. The table setting should be equally lively, easy to manage; slightly unconventional, if you choose—nothing to inhibit conversation. Top quality paper plates and napkins are a consideration—so easy to dispose of afterwards when you're eager to be off and running once again.

Just don't forget the flowers. Aries is the sign of spring. Great riotous masses of blossoms are a must. They symbolize the birthday kid so well—bold new colors after the barren winter.

Sometimes brash, often rash—but always young, always full of exciting promise.

ARIES — Spring Brunch for 20

♈ ♈ ♈ ♈ ♈ ♈ ♈ ♈ ♈ ♈ ♈ ♈

Mimosas

Skewers of Bacon, Chicken Liver, Sausage, Mushrooms,
Water Chestnuts, Tomatoes, Peppers, Onions

Cheese and Chili Squares

Croissants with Crème Suisse – Sweet Butter – Preserves

Grapefruit Salad with Mint Lime Dressing

Mocha Mousse
Espresso and Cappucino

♈ ♈ ♈ ♈ ♈ ♈ ♈ ♈ ♈ ♈ ♈ ♈

Aries Party Plan

Day before	Skewer the brochettes
	Make the chili cheese squares
	Whip up the crème suisse
	Slice grapefruits and make dressing
	Make mocha mousse
Early morning	Arrange the butter, preserves
	Arrange the salad
	Decorate the mousse
	Grind coffee beans and set up espresso maker
During brunch	Mix mimosas
	Broil or barbeque the skewers
	Heat squares and croissants
	Make espresso and cappucino

ᛉᛉᛉ Mimosas ᛉᛉᛉ

Approximately 6 bottles chilled champagne (it need not be too expensive)

3 quarts chilled fresh orange juice
Thin slices of orange

Mix champagne and orange in champagne flutes and garnish the side of the glass with an orange slice.

ᛉᛉᛉ Brunch Skewers ᛉᛉᛉ

Choose from the following:
2 lb thick bacon, cut into short lengths
2 lb cleaned and halved chicken livers
20 breakfast sausages, cut into 2" pieces
40 firm cleaned mushrooms
40 whole water chestnuts
40 cherry tomatoes
4 red or green peppers, cut into chunks
1 large red onion, with layers separated, cut into 1" pieces

Spear your chosen ingredients on long metal skewers. If using wooden skewers, use 2 for each brochette (this helps in turning them), soak them in water first, and wrap the ends in foil. The bacon could be wrapped around the chicken livers or water chestnuts. Sprinkle with black pepper and refrigerate.

Broil or barbecue, turning once or twice until the meats are cooked through.

4 T butter

2 8-oz cans diced green chilies

16 eggs

1 pint ricotta cheese

1 cup baking mix

2 cups milk or half and half

2 t baking powder

1 t salt

1 t or more hot sauce to taste

3-4 T chopped cilantro

8 oz grated Monterey jack cheese

8 oz grated cheddar cheese

Sour cream and cilantro leaves for garnish

Butter well two 9"x13" pans and spread the chilies evenly on the bottom. Mix the rest of the ingredients except the cheeses together and pour over the chilies. Sprinkle on the cheeses and bake at 350° for 30 minutes, until set and golden brown. Cut into squares. Top each one with a little sour cream and cilantro leaves and serve hot.

To serve later, reheat the ungarnished squares either in a 350° oven for 8-10 minutes or in a microwave on high for a minute or two.

12 oz good quality cream cheese
1/4 cup powdered sugar
1 T vanilla
2-3 T liqueur, e.g., orange liqueur or kirsch
3/4 cup whipping cream
20 freshly baked croissants
Sweet butter
Assortment of preserves and jams

Cream the cheese, sugar, vanilla and liqueur together until light. Whip the cream to the soft peak stage and fold into the cheese mixture. Chill well. For a slightly less calorific version, substitute low fat ricotta cheese and reduce the quantity of the whipping cream.

Using a butter curler, make curls of the sweet butter, arrange them in a dish and chill well. Wrap the croissants in foil and heat gently in the oven before serving.

ARIES

8-10 grapefruits
3-4 heads Belgian endive
1/2 cup walnut oil
Salt, pepper, and a pinch of dry mustard
1 t sugar
Juice of 3 limes
2-3 T freshly chopped mint
Lime slices and mint leaves for garnish

Remove the grapefruit skins with a serrated knife in a circular motion, taking care to remove all the pith. Neatly slice the fruit into thin circles. Mix all the dressing ingredients and adjust the seasoning if necessary. To serve, arrange the endive leaves around the outside of a large platter, arrange the grapefruit slices neatly on top in an overlapping pattern and pour over the dressing. Garnish with lime slices and mint leaves.

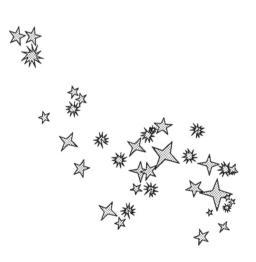

♈♈♈ *Mocha Mousse* ♈♈♈

2 cups small marshmallows

1 1/2 cups half and half

1 lb mocha flavored chocolate or white chocolate and 1 t
   coffee essence

6 T instant coffee powder

8 egg yolks

1/2 cup kahlua

8 egg whites

1 1/4 cups sugar

1 1/4 cups whipping cream

Garnish suggestions: Whipped cream rosettes, chocolate covered coffee beans, grated or curled chocolate.

Gently melt the marshmallows, half and half, chocolate and coffee together in a double boiler until completely smooth. This can also be done in a microwave, but be careful not to burn the chocolate. While still hot, beat in the egg yolks and kahlua. Cool. Beat the egg whites and 2 T of the sugar until thick and then beat in the remaining sugar to form a stiff meringue. Whip the cream until it forms peaks. Fold the meringue and the cream carefully into the cooled coffee mixture and turn into individual glasses or bowls to set. Garnish before serving.

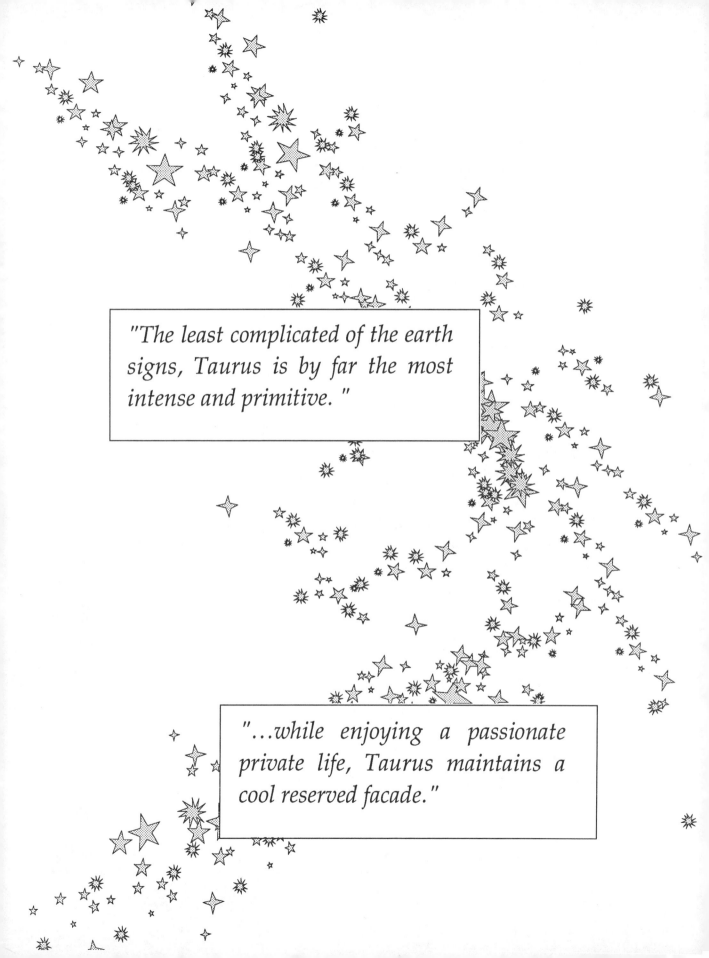

"The least complicated of the earth signs, Taurus is by far the most intense and primitive."

"...while enjoying a passionate private life, Taurus maintains a cool reserved facade."

TAURUS
A Backyard Barbeque on the Grand Scale for 10

Fresh Fruit Daiquiris

Iced Cucumber Soup with Mint

Barbequed Beef with Red Pepper Relish
Potatoes Savoyarde
French Bean Salad with Hazelnuts

Lemon Strawberry Tart

TAURUS

April 20 – May 20

Did you ever stop to think that the Taurus symbol of the bull is just another form of Dionysus, the wine loving fertility god ? Such a fun association and you do delight in making the most of it.

The least complicated of the earth signs, Taurus is by far the most intense and primitive. Your appreciation of the beauty and immediacy of the physical world is instinctive.

The strong macho symbol of the bull is ruled by Venus, the love goddess, who wants *so* much to please. Power in the world or power in bed? If you don't enjoy both, it's time you stopped sniffing the flowers and sharpened up those horns.

Really it's no surprise that the bull is the sign of the stockmarket. The best place to locate a Taurus——if not in a vineyard, farm or florist shop — would be in a real estate office, brokerage or bank. The key lies in your favorite color: green. Green as in plants, pasture and *money*.

Isn't it fortunate that you and money have such a good thing going because those luxurious tastes of yours simply demand it? You're just as fond of elegance as Leo. The only difference being that—for you—things must not only look good, but feel good as well. Behind that slow moving, indolent manner is one of the most sensuous of signs.

The Taurus man, for all the raging masculinity, takes a surprising amount of time perfecting his image: the right shoes, the appropriate shirt, hair just so, fingernails neat, a dash of aftershave. Behind the super jock facade, he, too, feels the Venus touch and wants very much to please.

The Taurean woman, whether a pampered, indolent love goddess or an earth mother type, shares that passion. Check out her bathroom. Note the oils, herbs, elixirs. Cleopatra would feel totally at home there. Then take a long look at her kitchen — a real mantrap if ever there was one.

Both Taureans prefer to read about food, sex and money—not always in that order. Does this all sound a trifle lightweight? Pleasure oriented—definitely. But shallow? Never! Ecology articles will be as well thumbed—as the financial pages. Taurus is nothing if not a nature–lover–conservationist. This extremely aesthetic sign is also highly knowledgeable about both art and music and will insist upon owning the best stereophonic equipment, paintings and sculpture.

What all this really means is that, while enjoying a passionate private life, Taurus maintains a cool reserved facade. Inside, she/he is thinking all the time.

Here is a sign with the relentless determination to pursue an idea or subject to its farthest conclusion. The profound and incredibly prolific William Shakespeare is a classic example. And when it comes to weighty enigmas, Taurus shows no reluctance to lock horns with the seeming imponderables. Only consider Immanuel Kant, J. Robert Oppenheimer and Teilhard de Chardin.

Would it surprise anyone to know that Sigmund Freud was a Taurus? Can't you just hear him? "Lie back on the couch and tell me all about it." You can be sure that couch was an extra comfy one. Naturally his own chair was well cushioned as he listened to a litany of earthy facts and fantasies.

One day it all came together for him or maybe he'd simply heard enough and wanted to expound his *own* ideas for a change. Whatever the case, the world has never been quite the same since.

Never, never, *never* underestimate the power of a Taurus!

A Backyard Barbecue on the Grand Scale

Kubla Khan must have been a Taurus. The fabled pleasure dome could only have been the creation of such a grand manner voluptuary.

Since this discriminating sign will settle for nothing but the best, an invitation to a Taurean soirée constitutes a compliment as well as carte blanche to sheer indulgence.

Sight: The Taurean home is a visual delight. While his/her dream house resembles Tara——plenty of trees, sloping lawns and flowering gardens, it's amazing what this sign can do with merely a patio or deck. Inside the house, expect a veritable feast of paintings, sculpture, wall hangings.

Sound: A surprising variety, and as always with Taurus, the best of the best. Background music provided by a medley of talented Taureans could include Bing Crosby, Ella Fitzgerald, Peter Tchaikovsky, Irving Berlin, Duke Ellington, Johannes Brahms, or Liberace.

Touch: Deep, rich rugs and couches, luxurious fur throws, silken pillows and soft velvety fabrics.

Smell: Exotic perfumes, fragrant flowers, but more exciting—the aroma of fantastic food being prepared by an expert who lives to eat rather than the reverse.

Now a detour. Before sampling the fifth of the senses—what about the collector of all those exquisite creature comforts? Are you anticipating someone just a bit bovine? Slightly heavy–footed? Ponderous, perhaps? Don't count on it.

Some of the most famous Taureans have amassed fortunes based on fancy footwork alone. Consider: Fred Astaire, Margot Fonteyn, Willy Mays, Sugar Ray Robinson. Audrey Hepburn began her career in ballet; today her image remains the personification of ethereal elegance. As for verbal gymnastics, could anyone be more outrageous than Bertrand Russell—unless, perhaps, it's Shirley MacLaine.

Now at long last, *taste*. Naturally it will be fantastic. Happiest always on her/his home turf, Taurus will choose a barbecue. If that conjures up notions of ketchup bottles and hot dogs—think again. When this sign decides to entertain close friends—the only variety Taurus bothers with—he/she goes all out.

You'll sense the ambience of luxury and comfort immediately just as surely as your senses grasp the other qualities that make up the Taurean lifestyle.

You'll enjoy cocktails in the garden or on the deck. Then step inside to the elegant dining area. The table draped in emerald green linen will be a perfect backdrop for a profusion of lilacs cascading from an exquisite vase, for the delicate china, the gleaming silver. The wine, carefully selected by the sign that does it best, will be served in sparkling crystal.

As you reach for your goblet, the sound of yet another Taurean star, Barbara Streisand, may be heard singing softly in the background ... "People who need people are the luckiest people in the world"... Sinking into your comfortable chair, you realize that you're one of the luckiest to be among *this* group of people.

Breathing a contented sigh, you raise your glass in a toast to Dionysus and Venus. The rites of earthly delight are about to begin.

TAURUS — Backyard Barbeque on the Grand Scale for 10

♉ ♉ ♉ ♉ ♉ ♉ ♉ ♉ ♉ ♉ ♉ ♉ ♉ ♉ ♉ ♉ ♉

Fresh Fruit Daiquiris

Iced Cucumber Soup with Mint

Barbequed Beef with Red Pepper Relish
Potatoes Savoyarde
French Bean Salad with Hazelnuts

Lemon Strawberry Tart

♉ ♉ ♉ ♉ ♉ ♉ ♉ ♉ ♉ ♉ ♉ ♉ ♉ ♉ ♉ ♉ ♉

Taurus Party Plan

The day before:	Make up the soup Marinate the meat Make the relish Make dessert but wait to decorate it
Before guests arrive:	Assemble the potato dish Make the bean salad Prepare the barbeque Decorate the dessert
During the barbeque:	Mix the daiquiris Barbeque the meat

♉ TAURUS

♉ ♉ ♉ *Fresh Fruit Daiquiris* ♉ ♉ ♉

5 fresh peaches or 2 cartons berries or 5 bananas
1 cup frozen lime concentrate or daiquiri mix
Juice of 5 fresh limes
2 cups rum
5-6 cups crushed ice

Mint sprigs and fruit to garnish

Make the daiquiris in several batches in a blender. Purée all ingredients thoroughly, pour into chilled wine glasses and decorate with appropriate fruit slices and mint sprigs.

♉ ♉ ♉ *Iced Cucumber Soup with Mint* ♉ ♉ ♉

3 oz butter
2 finely chopped onions
2-3 cloves garlic
4-5 European cucumbers
4 T flour
4-5 cups good chicken stock
Handful of fresh mint, finely chopped
2 cups half and half
2 cups plain yogurt
Salt and freshly ground white pepper

Reserve half of one cucumber and slice it very thinly for the garnish. Melt the butter in a large pan and sauté the onion and garlic until limp but not brown. Add the rest of the cucumbers, peeled and roughly chopped, and cook slowly until soft. Sprinkle on the flour, cook for a minute or two and then stir in the stock. Bring to a boil and then simmer for about 10 minutes. Cool, and then blend the soup in batches in a blender or food processor until completely smooth. Stir in the mint and chill well.

Just before serving, stir in the yogurt and half and half, and season with salt and pepper to taste. Garnish each serving with a swirl of half and half, and thinly sliced cucumbers.

♉

TAURUS

♉ ♉ ♉ *Barbequed Beef with Red Pepper Relish* ♉ ♉ ♉

About 6-7 lbs good quality beef of your choice, e.g., chateaubriand, sirloin steaks, etc.

Marinade:
1 cup red wine
1 cup soy sauce
Plenty of coarsely ground black pepper
Several cloves of garlic, crushed
About 2-3" of ginger root, peeled and chopped
1 cup tomato paste

Red Pepper Relish:
3 red peppers
1 bunch green onions, sliced
1 green or yellow pepper
2 T peanut oil
Salt and pepper to taste
1 T cumin
1/2 cup chopped cilantro
Juice of 2 limes

Mix all of the marinade ingredients, and cover the meat. Store overnight in the refrigerator.

To make the relish, chop the peppers into fine dice and sauté over high heat in the oil with the onions. Season with the salt, pepper and cumin, pour over the lime juice, and chill well.

Drain the meat and barbeque it, using the marinade as a basting liquid.

♉ ♉ ♉   *Potatoes Savoyarde*   ♉ ♉ ♉

2 lbs potatoes, white or russet
2-3 oz butter
Crushed garlic to taste
Salt and pepper
1 1/2 cups grated Gruyère cheese
About 1 1/2 cups beef stock

Peel and slice the potatoes and store them in cold water. Drain and dry them, and fry them in butter with the garlic to taste until they begin to turn golden. Lay them overlapping in a buttered ovenproof dish, seasoning with salt, pepper and cheese between layers. Finish with a neatly arranged overlapping ring of potatoes, pour over the stock and bake at 400° for about an hour, until well browned and cooked through.

This dish could be reheated for the party in a microwave oven.

♉ ♉ ♉ *French Bean and Hazelnut Salad* ♉ ♉ ♉

1 - 1 1/2 lbs fresh green beans
1/2 cup shelled hazelnuts
2 T dijon mustard
Juice of a lemon
1/4 cup cream
Salt, pepper and 2 T chopped tarragon

Clean the beans and cook them briefly in boiling water until barely tender. Plunge them immediately into a bowl of ice water to stop the cooking.

Slice the hazelnuts and lightly toast them under the broiler. Mix the dressing ingredients, and just before serving, toss the dried beans in the dressing, and sprinkle over the nuts.

♉ ♉ ♉ *Lemon Strawberry Tart* ♉ ♉ ♉

2 cups flour
6 oz butter
1/4 cup sugar
Ice water or beaten egg to bind
12 oz cream cheese
3/4 cup sugar
Grated rind and juice of 2 lemons
3 eggs

2 cartons fresh strawberries (or other fresh fruit, e.g.,
   cherries, raspberries, etc.)

Beat the flour, butter and sugar in a food processor until crumbly and add just enough egg or water so that it begins to bind together. Press into the bottom of a large fluted flan case with a removable bottom. Support the sides with strips of crumpled foil and bake at 400° for about 10 minutes.

Meanwhile, beat the cheese with the sugar until creamy, then add lemon rind and juice, and eggs. Pour into the half-cooked pastry case, and bake at 325° until just setting, about 20 minutes. Cool well.

Clean the berries and slice neatly in half. Arrange them very carefully over the top of the tart.

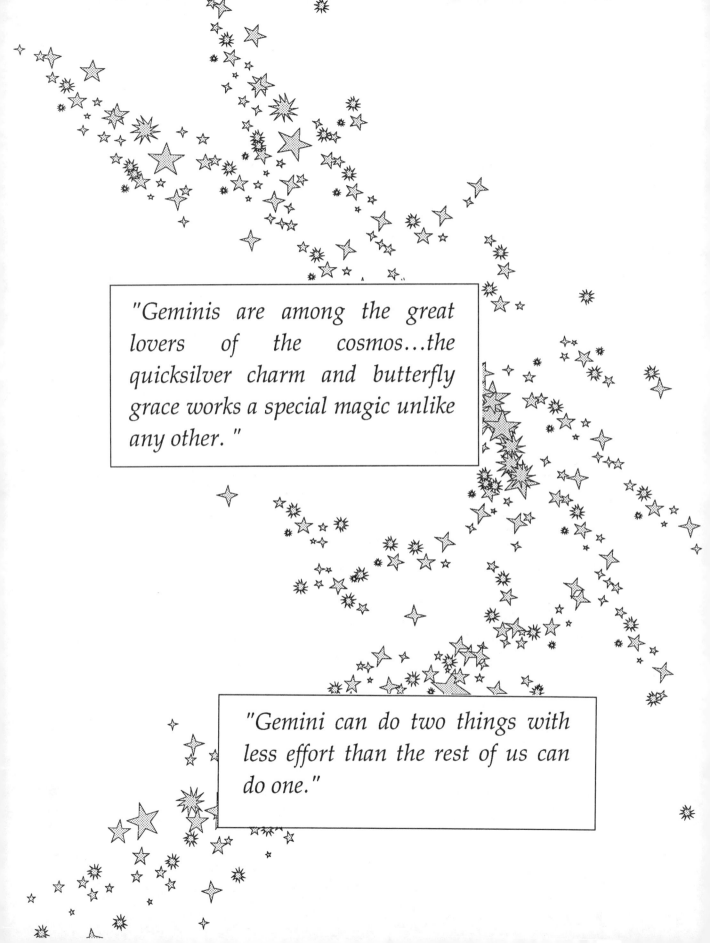

"Geminis are among the great lovers of the cosmos...the quicksilver charm and butterfly grace works a special magic unlike any other."

"Gemini can do two things with less effort than the rest of us can do one."

GEMINI
A Wine Tasting on
Cleopatra's Pleasure Barge

Variety of Chosen Wines for Tasting

Cheeseboard with Apples, French Bread
Spiced Nuts

Layered Fish Terrine
Horseradish Sauce
Sliced Ham and Cumberland Sauce
Marinated Colored Peppers

Grand Marnier Peach Cream

GEMINI

May 21-June 20

Geminis—speak for yourselves. Nobody does it better.

Isadora Duncan writes her memoirs: "How to begin? Is it to be Chaste Madonna, or Messalina, or the Magdalen or the Blue Stocking? It seems to me that there was not one but hundreds and my soul soaring aloft, not really affected by any of them."

Walt Whitman: "Do I contradict myself … I contain multitudes."

Al Jolson: "Folks, you ain't heard *nothing* yet!"

Whether they realized it or not, each of these Geminis caught the essence of their cosmic character. The traditional symbol of the twins is a trifling understatement. The true Gemini emblem is a brilliant butterfly, darting here and there momentarily revealing a profusion of colorful possibilities.

The individual who snares this dazzling creature can expect a veritable army to please her or a harem to pleasure him. But since turnabout is only fair—the challenge is very clear. Tired already? Poor dear.

Besides versatility, Geminis have a snappy line of patter. Count on them to be the liveliest of conversationalists. Not always right, of course; but they *sound* fantastic! Who can resist such an outpouring of wit, effervescence and creativity?

Perhaps that's why Geminis are among the great lovers of the cosmos. Just consider Errol Flynn, Marilyn Monroe, Rudolph Valentino; or even more intriguing: Ian Fleming (creator of James Bond), Brigham Young (creator of the American harem), and Wallis Simpson (creator of a duke who might have been a king.)

It might be asking too much to expect such bigger than life *grandes amoreuses* to forgo flirting, charming, cajoling, teasing, persuading or just plain entertaining everyone who happens into their orbit. Geminis belong to the world.

Since everybody knows that a Gemini can do two things with less effort than the rest of us can do one—a double life is almost inevitable. Only think of John F. Kennedy. Marvel at his ingenuity—not to mention stamina.

Of course it doesn't have to be two (or more) physical loves that exert that perennial pull. It could be career conflicts, a covey of causes, a plentitude of projects. For Gemini, more is always better.

Whichever the direction and there will be several, Gemini has a passion for novelty—a fresh shoulder to cry on, a different puzzle to ponder, a new world to conquer—the quicksilver charm and butterfly grace works a special magic unlike any other. Where does reality end and illusion begin? With Gemini, of course.

Theirs is the psychedelic light show in the dark discotheque of life. Who wants to mess around with one little candle when you can have a shot at that?

air sign

Wine Tasting and Picnic on the Water for 10
(A Wine Tasting On Cleopatra's Pleasure Barge)

Who but another Gemini would take on F. Lee Bailey in a verbal joust?

The blithe spirit of the cosmos, Mercury's child of enchantment exudes charm from every pore but possesses a keen and ready wit as well.

The consummate communicator, no conversational challenge would be too great. Surely Scheherazade was a Gemini. Can't you just see her, long tapering fingers pushing back a strand of raven hair as she reclines on the Sultan's couch weaving her delicate ethereal magic night after night? Small wonder that she became his number one talk show for life.

Every hostess's dream, this is the party kid of the cosmos, never tiring of gaiety and gossip. A past master/mistress of small talk, Gemini can be counted on to keep things light and frothy.

Super sophisticated, here's one sign with more than a touch of class. Just think of David Niven (a Gemini playing a Gemini) in *Around the World in 80 Days*. Remember the casual manner in which he leaned out of his balloon scooping up a little Alpine snow to cool his champagne?

When Isadora Duncan—a classic Gemini—flipped for Issac Singer she immediately replaced his name with the more romantic, Lohengrin. "Lohengrin" (Probably a plan-ahead Virgo) knew his lady well. Too much togetherness would have popped their bubble. Instead he swooped up Isadora and about 100 of her most intimate friends and took them all sailing up the Nile for a house party that lasted for months.

This kind of gala was tailormade to the sign that likes its love and adventure on the grand scale—with a built in escape hatch, of course. There's something about a Gemini that calls to mind a dashing riverboat gambler, wit facile as his fingers as he flips through the deck. The fate of a plantation may ride on the turn of a card. Does Gemini worry? Not for a moment. His manner is lively, nonchalant—the casual cool of one who knows exactly where his next ace is buried.

Or slipping deeper still into fantasy land (Gemini's magic kingdom), imagine Cleopatra's pleasure barge. Now there's the ultimate party pad. Yacht, sailboat, motorboat, even a rowboat—leave it to a Gem to create the ambience of an elegant orgy.

Besides talking and flirting, the main event will be a wine tasting—yet another opportunity to satisfy the birthday kid's passion for variety and change.

For a color scheme, consider the hot pinks, mauves, muted maroons, blues and greens of that romantic roamer, Paul Gauguin.

Naturally the favorite sound of any Gemini is that of corks popping; but additional background music can be supplied by tapes of another astral sibling, the restless rainbow girl, Judy Garland, or what about Cole Porter.

Ummmm, can't you hear it now?   "Night and Day," "I've Got you Under My Skin," "You do Something to Me". . . . . .Rarely does a Gemini bare his/her soul, but when it happens, it's wonderful.

What a party!

GEMINI – Wine Tasting and Picnic on the Water for 10

♊ ♊ ♊ ♊ ♊ ♊ ♊ ♊ ♊ ♊ ♊ ♊ ♊ ♊

Variety of Chosen Wines for Tasting

Cheeseboard with Apples, French Bread
Spiced Nuts

Layered Fish Terrine
Horseradish Sauce
Sliced Ham and Cumberland Sauce
Marinated Colored Peppers

Grand Marnier Peach Cream

♊ ♊ ♊ ♊ ♊ ♊ ♊ ♊ ♊ ♊ ♊ ♊ ♊ ♊

Gemini Party Plan

Day before:	Spice the nuts Make the terrine and sauce and chill Marinate the peppers Slice the ham and make the cumberland sauce Make the dessert and refrigerate to set Chill the wines
Before leaving:	Pack the picnic basket
On the boat :	Arrange the cheeses and nuts Slice the terrine and garnish the platter Arrange the ham plate and the peppers Unmold and decorate the dessert Set up wines and glasses for tasting

♊♊♊ *Spiced Nuts* ♊♊♊

1 lb of fresh pecan or walnut halves (or both)

Recipe 1:

        4 T butter
        2 T good curry powder

Recipe 2:

        4 T butter
        1 T chili powder
        1 t ground cumin
        1 t ground coriander
        Salt to taste

Recipe 3:

        4 T olive oil
        4 T chopped fresh basil
        4 T chopped fresh parsley
        1 clove garlic
        Salt and pepper to taste
        Parmesan cheese to sprinkle on when cold
        (optional)

Blanch the nuts in boiling water for a minute or two and then toast them in a 350° oven until just turning color, about 10 minutes. Choose your recipe, heat the oil or butter in a frying pan and sauté the nuts. Then add other spice ingredients, turning in the pan until the nuts are well covered. Drain on paper towels and store in an airtight container.

♊♊♊ *Layered Fish Terrine* ♊♊♊

1 1/2 lbs fresh sole fillets
3/4 lb fresh scallops
3 eggs
1 1/2 cups fresh breadcrumbs
Salt and white pepper
Pinch garlic salt
2 T white wine vinegar
2 cups heavy cream

Green layer:
1 bunch finely chopped green onions
1/2 bunch spinach leaves, or 1 bunch watercress
Few tablespoons chopped parsley
Little butter for cooking

Red layer:
1/2 lb smoked salmon, or 1/2 lb shrimp and 1 small jar
diced pimento
2 T tomato paste

A food processor is almost essential to grind the fish smoothly. Grind the sole and the scallops until smooth and then add eggs, crumbs, and seasonings. With the motor running, pour in the cream. Divide this mousse into three equal portions. Sauté the onions, spinach or watercress and parsley in a little butter, and add to one third of the mousse. Purée until smooth. Process another portion with the salmon or shrimp and pimento, and tomato. Butter an oblong terrine pan and line the insides with buttered parchment paper. With a rubber spatula, spread in the layers, one after another, smoothing them out evenly. Cover with foil and bake in a water bath in a 350° oven for at least an hour until set. Cool well and unmold. Serve with slices of lemon and horseradish sauce.

♊♊♊ *Horseradish Sauce* ♊♊♊

3/4 cup sour cream
3 T mayonnaise
1 T freshly grated or prepared horseradish
Salt, pepper and lemon juice to taste
3 T chopped fresh chives

Mix all ingredients together until smooth and chill.

♊♊♊ *Sliced Ham and Cumberland Sauce* ♊♊♊

1 pre-roasted honey-baked ham
2 oranges
1 lemon
1 1/2 cups red currant jelly
1/2 cup port
1 t ground ginger
Salt and pepper

Using a grater or a zester, remove the rinds of the oranges and lemon and chop into small pieces. Bring the jelly, port and seasonings to a gentle boil, and whisk until perfectly smooth. Add the juice and rinds of the oranges and lemon. Chill and serve cold with the sliced ham.

♊♊♊ *Marinated Colored Peppers* ♊♊♊

4 or 5 peppers of different colors, e.g., red, green yellow,
   orange or purple
3-4 T olive oil
1 clove crushed garlic
Black pepper and salt to taste
2 T balsamic vinegar
Juice of 1 lemon
1/2 t paprika

Clean the peppers and cut them into even stick shapes. Sauté the garlic in olive oil, and toss the peppers in the pan to half cook them, still retaining their crispness. Add the seasoning ingredients. Chill well before serving.

♊♊♊ *Grand Marnier Peach Cream* ♊♊♊

4-5 ripe peaches
3/4 cup sugar
Pinch allspice
1 packet gelatine
1/4 cup Grand Marnier
2 egg yolks
3 T sugar
1 t vanilla
1 cup whipped cream
Fresh fruits for decoration

Peel the peaches and mash them with the sugar until smooth. Sprinkle the gelatine over the Grand Marnier in a small pan, and when it has been absorbed, heat gently until smooth. Stir into the peaches. Beat the yolks, sugar and vanilla until thick and light. Fold this into the peach mixture, followed by the whipped cream. Turn into a ring mold to chill and set. Unmold onto a dampened platter (so that it can be slid across the plate if necessary) and garnish with fresh fruits, e.g., cherries, strawberries, kiwi, peach slices.

GEMINI

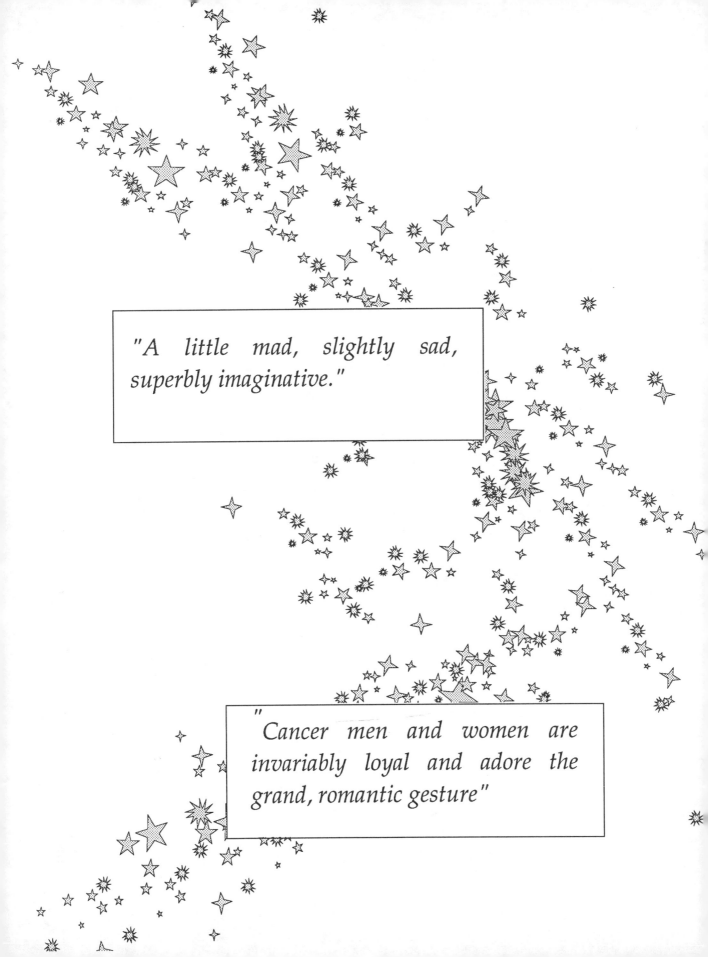

"A little mad, slightly sad, superbly imaginative."

"Cancer men and women are invariably loyal and adore the grand, romantic gesture"

CANCER
An Old Fashioned Fourth of July Picnic

Cranberry Punch

Tropical Coolers

Crab Salad Baguettes
Honey Glazed Chicken
Potato Salad
Avocado Melon Salad

Apple Peach Pie

CANCER

June 2l-July 22

A little mad, slightly sad, superbly imaginative, Cancer the cosmic moonchild, is a study in contradiction.

The classic "roots" sign, Cancers are enthralled with the past and guaranteed to know every branch of the family tree down to the tiniest twig. More than a little conservative, they cling to tradition and possessions with typical crab-like tenacity. If it was good enough for Grandma, it's still good enough—including that broken chair stored in the attic.

Moonchildren save *everything:* old teddy bears, merit badges, prom corsages, love letters—well, of course love letters! But there's also a practical side to this super sentimentalist. Gemini saves clippings, but if Cancer clips anything it'll be coupons on tax exempt bonds. Besides old tintypes and grammar school art, there are costly antiques, sculpture and valuable paintings—all readily convertible to cash.

If a male Cancer invites you to see his etchings, he really *has* etchings and they'll be well worth viewing. In addition to memorabilia, Moonchildren collect property, T bills, and bank books. It isn't surprising that the original John D. Rockefeller was a Cancer along with Nelson and assorted other Rockefellers.

What could a crab and a bull have in common? Between them, Cancer and Taurus control most of the world's wealth. Both share a penchant for the good life and a love of greenery—the kind found in flower pots and bank vaults. Moonmaidens are prone to basic black and pearls; as the years pass, the pearls are more and more likely to be real. You can be certain that both sexes prefer their wallets to be pleasingly plump.

Male and female Cancers are inclined to deify Mother. And neither are the least amused by mother-in-law jokes.   It should come as no surprise that artist James Whistler was a Cancerian.   Yet another moonchild, Virginia Satir, was the "mother" of family therapy, a concept she introduced on a global scale and Cancerian twins, Ann Landers and Abigail van Buren, are mother confessors to the world. Home is definitely where the heart is for this sign. Moonkid Stephen Foster even wrote a song about it, "My Old Kentucky Home."

Just recall Olivia de Haviland (a Cancer) in the role of Melanie Wilkes—the consummate moonmaid. Could anyone be sweeter, gentler, more devoted to family, children, tradition than Melanie? But remember, she was also ready and willing to defend it all with a sword if necessary. No one takes *anything* away from a Cancer!

Like Melanie, Cancer men and women are invariably loyal and adore the grand, romantic gesture—like the Duke of Windsor, naturally a Cancer, giving up his throne for the woman he loved. They wallow in soft words, sweet caresses.   The women overtly, the man secretly, have a thing for romantic novels. *Romeo and Juliet* or its most modern update, *Love Story*, are soul food.

Nancy Reagan is typical.   In her girlhood fantasies she'd envisioned herself with a suitor who'd serenade her in a canoe, accompanying himself on a ukulele. Then as she reclined, one hand trailing languidly in the water, he'd propose.   It didn't happen that way and she never forgot it—nor did she allow Ronnie to forget. Finally on their 25th wedding anniversary, Nancy's dream came true. Her air sign husband finally got the message and presented her with a canoe christened "Tru Luv."   As they paddled forth on the lake of their ranch, she forgave him for possessing neither a ukulele or a singing voice and allowed that it would be okay if he just hummed.

Cancers usually translate all that emotional outpouring into very practical terms. They are fantastic cooks, the great chefs and restaurateurs of the world.

Family, food and money are always primary concerns. Isn't it intriguing that Ernest Hemingway, for all his macho, his chest thumping wanderlust, never for a moment attempted to go it alone. Like all moonchildren, he desperately needed someone to nurture, protect and spoil—with corresponding reciprocity. There was a man who not only adored cooking for his friends but insisted that they call him "Papa." There was also a man whose literary themes were deeply symbolic.

The moon rules the instincts and intuition as well as the emotions. Its children—beyond the family oriented facade—have a rich secret side, a mysterious inner world that often leads to grand adventures.

Frequently a slow maturing sign (the women rarely emerge from the kitchen-nursery until at least 35) they respond to lunar magic in surprising ways.

The moon can be a highly creative midwife. Only to think of the richly symbolic, mythic and mystical works of Proust, Hesse, Chagall and Ingmar Bergman.   P.T. Barnum turned his love of children, money and fantasy into a veritable circus. Henry Thoreau wrote of a "different drummer." John Glenn heard that faint tattoo and followed it. Where did it take him?

Right out of this world!

water sign

An Old Fashioned July 4th Picnic for 12

All Cancers are mothers at heart—including the men.

Each has a special gift for creating a warm, loving atmosphere and for dealing gently with emotional and physical bruises. No friend or family member will ever starve for food or affection. Cancerians, care deeply about the hungry and feel a personal responsibility toward every empty plate in the world.

Appropriately Nelson Rockefeller's campaign slogan, "I Care," was prominently displayed in supermarket entrances across the nation. Cancer rules the stomach and as such is the big food producer of the world.

No one should be too surprised that the United States falls under the sign (and spell) of Cancer. The Yankee Doodle baby, born on the fourth of July, knows exactly what's best for everyone. Who else would invent the CARE package? Here is the eternal mother lavishing everyone within reaching distance with food, money, medicine and advice. And again, like a mother, hurt, petulant and martyred when her largess is forgotten, her advice ignored. "Look at all I've done for you! What's the matter, don't you love me anymore?" What mother hasn't asked that one?

Like all Cancers, the U.S. Government remains powerless to resist the lunar pull. Weren't we the very first to land on the moon?

Cancers are invariably patriotic. They have an insatiable curiosity and fascination for the past and find historical figures nearly as intriguing as their own ancestors. It's only natural that Cancer would celebrate his/her natal day with a July 4th picnic. The observance of tradition by a gathering of the family and close friends who mean so much to the Moonchild is part of this sign's very special need for sharing and recognition.

You can be absolutely certain that the food will be superb and there'll be lots of it.   Plenty of second helpings—but be sure you clean your plate!

The ambience will be just a bit sentimental, the re-telling of family anecdotes, much fussing over new babies, engagements, weddings. Children will romp and play.   Lovers of all ages will wander off to stand by the water's edge.

Old favorites will be sung, very likely music by talented Moonkids, Oscar Hammerstein and Richard Rodgers.   Could anything be more traditionally American than the themes of *Oklahoma* or *South Pacific?*

Nellie Forbush ran the gamut of Moonchild traits: Loving, humorous, conventional, maternal, idealistic and a little crabby too.   And she said it all so well, "I'm as corny as Kansas in August, high as the flag on the 4th of July. . . ."

No July 4th festivity would be complete without fireworks.   For a Cancer they are a vibrant celebration of the continuity of life.   Other signs may secretly believe that their natal day should be a national holiday. For Moonchildren, it's a glorious reality!

CANCER

CANCER – An Old Fashioned Fourth of July Picnic for 12

Cranberry Punch

Tropical Coolers

Crab Salad Baguettes

Honey Glazed Chicken
Potato Salad
Avocado Melon Salad

Apple Peach Pie

Cancer Party Plan

The day before: Marinate the chicken
Make the potato salad
Make the apple peach pie

Before the picnic: Mix the tropical coolers
Make the crab salad baguettes
Assemble the avocado melon salad
Pack the coolers and baskets

At the picnic: Mix the punch
Slice the baguettes
Barbeque the chicken

ᑐᑐᑐ *Cranberry Punch (non-alcoholic)* ᑐᑐᑐ

1 quart cranberry juice
1 quart clear apple juice
Juice of 2 oranges, 2 lemons, 2 limes
1 quart sparkling water
1 quart ginger ale
Sliced citrus fruits and berries to float in punch
1 ice mold

To make the ice mold, place a bowl full of water with sliced fruit or berries or mint leaves in the freezer overnight. This will stay frozen at the picnic longer than ordinary ice.

Mix all ingredients together and float the fruit and ice mold.

ᑐᑐᑐ *Tropical Coolers* ᑐᑐᑐ

Kiwi mango cooler:
4 kiwi fruit
2 mangoes
1 cup canned cream of coconut
Juice of 4 lemons
1/4 cup sugar
4 cups crushed ice
(1 cup vodka optional extra)

Lime papaya cooler:
Grated rind and juice of 3 limes
4 papayas
1 banana
2 cups pineapple juice
1/2 cup cream of coconut
4 cups crushed ice
1/2 cup honey
(1 cup rum or vodka)

Prepare the fruits and blend all ingredients until smooth. Store in thermos containers and serve over ice at the picnic, garnished with appropriate fruits.

♋♋♋ *Crab Salad Baguettes* ♋♋♋

3 baguettes of French bread

Crisp inside leaves from 2 heads romaine

1 1/2 lbs crab meat (or imitation crab)

1 cup diced celery

1/2 cup finely chopped red onion

1 small can waterchestnuts, diced

1 cup mayonnaise

1 t tabasco

Salt, pepper and lemon juice to taste

Slice off the top 1/4 of each baguette and hollow out the bottoms. Line these with the lettuce leaves. Blend all of the crab salad ingredients together, and spread into the bread. Replace the tops and wrap the loaves tightly.

♋♋♋ *Honey Glazed Chicken* ♋♋♋

(This recipe works just as well with game hens or duck pieces)

About 24 portions of chicken of your choice

1 cup honey

3/4 cup dijon mustard

3 T ground ginger

3 T curry powder

About 1/2 cup soy sauce or red wine to achieve a paste
consistency

Salt, black pepper and garlic to taste

Marinate the chicken portions overnight in the honey paste. If you have a barbeque at the picnic, either pre-bake the chicken for about 20 minutes in a 350° oven and finish off over the charcoal (this helps to cook the inside of the chicken without burning the outside), or cook slowly over not too hot coals. If you do not have a barbeque, bake the chicken completely in a 350° oven (about 40 minutes) and serve hot or cold at the picnic.

♋♋♋ Red Potato Salad ♋♋♋

2 lbs small red potatoes
1/4 cup white wine vinegar
3/4 cup mayonnaise
2 T mustard
1/2 cup chopped green onions
1/2 European cucumber, neatly diced
1/2 cup chopped celery
Salt and pepper to taste
Plenty of chopped fresh mint, chives and parsley

Optional extras:
Add 4 chopped hardboiled eggs or 2 grated carrots or 1
diced green pepper
Sprinkle cooked crumbled bacon over the top

Scrub but do not peel the potatoes and cook them whole in simmering salted water. Chill them completely before slicing neatly. Mix the potatoes with the chopped vegetables and dressing ingredients, and refrigerate until serving time.

♋♋♋ *Melon Avocado Salad* ♋♋♋

    2 or 3 ripe melons of your choice, preferably green and
      orange
    3-4 ripe avocados
    1 carton cherry tomatoes
    1 cup red or green grapes

Poppyseed dressing:
    2 bananas
    12 oz plain yogurt
    2 T poppyseeds
    2-3 T honey

Using a melon baller, scoop out the melon and avocados. Purèe the bananas completely and mix with the yogurt, poppyseeds and honey, and toss the fruit and vegetables in the dressing. Chill well.

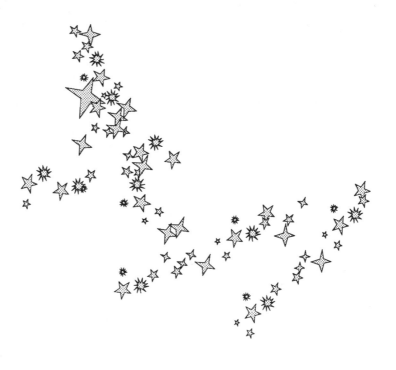

CANCER

᎒᎒᎒ *Apple Peach Pie* ᎒᎒᎒

2 lbs crisp apples
2 lbs fresh peaches
1 1/2 cup sugar
2 T cinnamon
Grated rind and juice of 1 lemon

3 cups flour
1 1/4 cups shortening
1 t salt
6 T ice water

2 oz butter
2 T sugar and cinnamon

Peel and slice the fruits and turn over in the cinnamon sugar and lemon juice.

Meanwhile, make the pastry by crumbling the flour and salt with the shortening, and lightly blending in just enough water to form a dough. Divide the dough into 2/3 and 1/3. Roll the larger piece out and line the bottom of 1 large or 2 small buttered pie pans. Add the fruit and dot with pieces of butter. Roll out the remainder of the dough and cut into 1" strips. Lay these in a lattice pattern over the fruit. Sprinkle oven the cinnamon sugar and bake for about 45 minutes until cooked through, when the pastry should be golden brown.

If you have a refrigerator near your picnic, serve the pie warm or cold with vanilla ice cream.

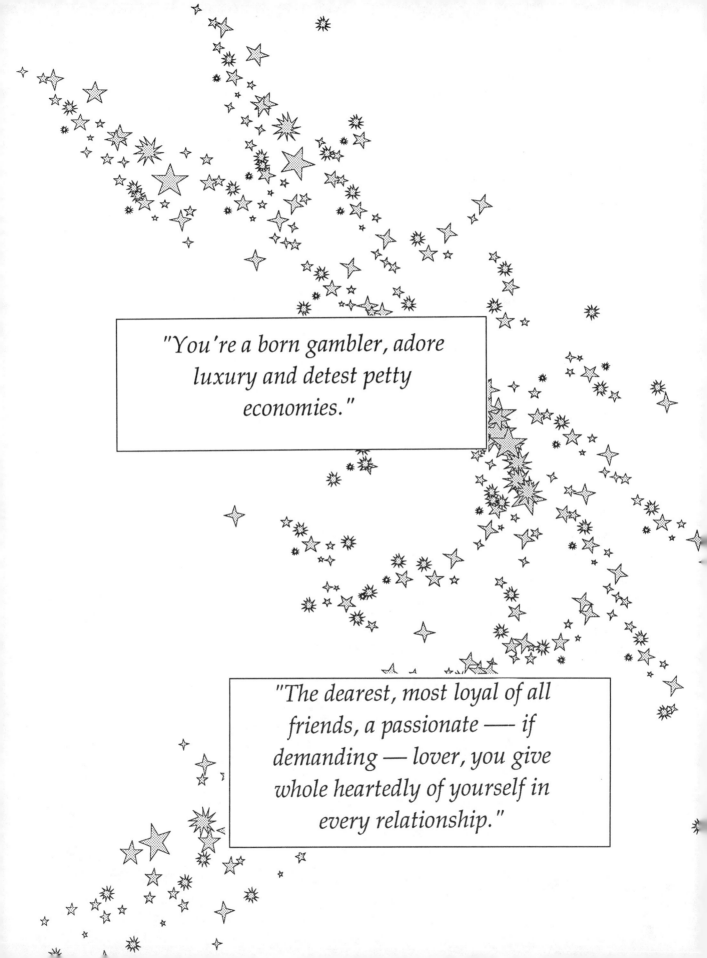

"You're a born gambler, adore luxury and detest petty economies."

"The dearest, most loyal of all friends, a passionate — if demanding — lover, you give whole heartedly of yourself in every relationship."

LEO
A Garden Party in the
Cecil B. De Mille Tradition

Crudités with Curry Dip
Smoked Salmon Canapés
Cheese Platter

Iced Shrimp and Avocado Gazpacho

Summer Chicken and Grape Salad
Spinach Salad
Hot Cheese Bread

Watermelon Basket of Fruit Skewers
Summer Fruit Meringues

LEO

July 23-August 22

Child of the glowing sun, you radiate an aura of courage and confidence that lights up the world. Both proud and magnanimous, it never occurs to you to hold back anything. You're splendidly generous with time, money and, ah, yes, advice. You *do* love to give advice.

Fortunately your ideas are generally very practical. You know exactly what works for you and others. Didn't Mussolini get the trains running on time? And Julia Child doesn't just tell us how to cook, she shows us, obviously adoring every minute of it.

That incandescent sizzle of yours sets you apart from the rest of us mere mortals. Expecting admiration as your due, you generally receive it. If not, you'll move to a more appreciate setting. Pick a pool and you're bound to be kingfish.

Though you detest the mundane details of daily living, you can be as home centered as a Moonchild; yet, for you, the effect is totally different. Home to Cancer is a haven, a psychological refuge. With you, it's more apt to be a repository of elegant comforts and a display case for your many achievements. You're a born gambler, adore luxury and detest petty economies. Would Princess Margaret take a bus? Hardly! Nor would another astral sibling, Princess Anne.

Your strength, your dynamism, your flamboyance are the side you show the world.   Inside—deep inside--there's a little … well, let's admit it, a little mush.   You're not really as self sufficient as you appear. It takes a lot of love to make your world go round. Fortunately, with your magnetic appeal, you'll have little difficulty obtaining it.

Vitality flows out to others who draw strength from you. The dearest, most loyal of all friends, a passionate—if demanding—lover, you give whole heartedly of yourself in every relationship.

The cosmos has dealt you a good hand.   You play it well.   The whole world wins.

fire sign

LEO'S Garden Gala

What do you want most in the world?

Taurus will answer money. Capricorn, prestige. Scorpio, the perfect lover.

You, proud Leo, not only want them all; but consider them your due. Naturally the sign that spawned Bonaparte, Castro, Mussolini and Jacqueline Onassis isn't going to be content with a casual get together.

Be honest, don't you secretly believe your natal day should be declared a national holiday? It's asking a lot to content yourself with merely the grandest bash in the book—a luncheon for fifty intimate friends—but the opportunity to bask in the sun, *your* sun, is too seductive to pass up.

As if you didn't know, the heavenly body associated with your sign is the power source that vitalizes the entire solar system. Annie Oakley is a prime example of the Leo desire for independence and the need to excel. Star of stage, screen and radio on the home front, it should come as no surprise to discover astral links with Cecil B. DeMille, Mae West, Mick Jagger, Lucille Ball, Alfred Hitchcock, John Huston, Robert DeNiro and Robert Redford.

In keeping with those show bizz proclivities, you may want to rent a marquee for your outdoor party. A champagne fountain would be a nice touch too. (Your secret mantra is MINO—an acronym for Money Is No Object). Consider hiring caterers. Being pampered appeals to that regal nature of yours and what better day to indulge? You owe it to yourself— and to your public.

LEO — A Garden Party Luncheon for 50

ഒ ഒ ഒ ഒ ഒ ഒ ഒ ഒ ഒ ഒ ഒ ഒ ഒ ഒ

Crudités with Curry Dip
Smoked Salmon Canapés

Cheese Platter
Iced Shrimp and Avocado Gazpacho

Summer Chicken and Grape Salad
Spinach Salad
Hot Cheese Bread

Watermelon Basket of Fruit Skewers
Summer Fruit Meringues

ഒ ഒ ഒ ഒ ഒ ഒ ഒ ഒ ഒ ഒ ഒ ഒ ഒ ഒ

Leo's Party Plan

The day before: Completely assemble the chicken salad
Make the dip
Carve the watermelon
Make the meringues

Before the party: Prepare the crudités and put them in ice
water before arranging
Make the salmon canapés
Arrange the cheese and crackers
Prepare bread for heating
Wash spinach and make dressing
Garnish the chicken
Skewer the fresh fruit
Whip cream and fill meringues

During the party: Let the "help" pass the appetizers, heat the
bread, toss the salad and serve.

ഇരരെ *Crudités with Curry Dip* ഇരരെ

Arrange a basket, lined with attractive greens, with a variety of fresh raw or barely blanched vegetables, cut into shapes for dipping. Try raw jicama slices, carrot sticks or rounds, celery, flowered radishes, flowerets of cauliflower, red, green and yellow pepper spears, cherry tomatoes, etc., and blanched asparagus spears, green beans, broccoli flowerets, etc. Serve with a favorite dip or use the following:

> *Curry dip:*
> 1/2 lb soft cream cheese
> 2/3 cup mayonnaise
> 1/3 cup sour cream
> 1 T curry powder

Mix all ingredients together until smooth, and season to taste if necessary.

ഇരരെ *Cheese Platter* ഇരരെ

Select three or four favorite cheeses and arrange on a large platter covered with fresh grape vine leaves. Serve with crackers or French bread, polished red apples and small bunches of black grapes.

තතත *Smoked Salmon Canapés* තතත

6-8 zucchini
1/2 lb soft cream cheese
1 lb sliced smoked salmon
Black caviar or dill sprigs or tiny lemon twists

Score the sides of the zucchini with a fork and slice then into 1/4" rounds. Spread neatly with the cream cheese and top with pieces of smoked salmon and chosen garnish.

තතත *Iced Shrimp and Avocado Gazpacho* තතත

6 one-quart bottles clam and tomato juice "clamato"
2 quarts tomato or V-8 juice
2 bunches thinly sliced green onions
1/2 cup olive oil
1/2 cup red wine vinegar
4 T sugar
3 T dill weed
4 crushed garlic cloves
1 T tabasco
2 T lemon juice
Salt and pepper to taste
1 T Worcestershire sauce
6 avocados, neatly diced
3 lbs cooked shrimp
3 peeled and neatly diced European cucumbers

Assemble all the ingredients and chill overnight. Recheck the seasoning. The shrimp will turn bright pink.

෯෯෯ Summer Chicken and Grape Salad ෯෯෯

35-40 half chicken breasts
1 onion, 1 bay leaf, sprig parsley
2 lbs sliced waterchestnuts
5 bunches green onions
1/2 cup sesame oil
1/4 cup vinegar
3 cups mayonnaise
Salt and freshly ground pepper to taste
Chopped chives for garnish

In a very large pan, poach the chicken breasts in water or stock with the seasonings until tender, about 20-30 minutes. Cool, preferably in the poaching liquid to keep the chicken moist. Remove the skin and bones, and shred the chicken into fairly large pieces.

Slice the onions, separate the grapes, reserving a few bunches for garnish, and mix these with the chicken, waterchestnuts, oil, vinegar, mayonnaise, salt and pepper. Chill well and top with chives and small bunches of grapes.

෯෯෯ Hot Cheese Bread ෯෯෯

6 loaves freshly baked French bread
6 sticks of butter
Garlic salt (or freshly crushed garlic)
Parmesan cheese
Paprika

Slice the bread lengthways and spread with the butter. Sprinkle with the garlic, cheese and paprika. Heat for about 10 minutes in a 350° oven. Slice into 2" portions for serving.

৯৯৯ *Spinach Salad* ৯৯৯

10-15 bunches of fresh spinach, depending on the size
1 1/2 lbs bacon
2 lbs mushrooms, cleaned and sliced
6 shallots, finely chopped
3 cloves minced garlic
2 cups olive oil
1 cup red wine vinegar
2 T dijon mustard
4 T Worcestershire sauce
1 T curry powder
4 T brandy
1 T sugar
Salt and freshly ground black pepper to taste
6 hard boiled eggs (optional)
Alfalfa or clover sprouts

Wash the spinach carefully to remove all traces of grit. Tear into pieces and dry. Then place in bags and refrigerate until serving time.

Dice the bacon finely and fry until crisp; set aside. Remove most of the fat from the pan, and fry the mushrooms, shallots and garlic in the remainder. Mix the dressing ingredients and chop the eggs.

When ready to serve, toss the spinach, sprouts, mushrooms and shallots with the dressing and top with the bacon and eggs.

1 large watermelon
3 cantaloupes
3 lbs strawberries
3 fresh pineapples
10 bananas
2 lbs large black grapes
2 cups sliced coconut flakes
1 bunch white daisies

With a felt tip pen, draw a handle about 1 1/2" wide on the top of the watermelon and mark a line around it about one third of the way down. Carefully cut along the lines and then remove the two pieces that come away and all the flesh to leave a basket with a handle. Turn on one side to drain, being careful not to break the handle. Scallop or zig zag the edges of the basket.

Cut other fruit into chunks and place them into a large bowl of water with a few tablespoons of lemon juice to prevent browning. Just before the party, spear the fruit with wooden skewers and arrange them in the melon. Using toothpicks, pin strawberries and daisies to the basket and serve on a platter surrounded with sliced coconut flakes.

ಬಬಬ *Summer Fruit Meringues* ಬಬಬ

If you are short of time, buy meringues from a bakery, but for a fresher, softer texture, try this:

20-25 egg whites (about 3 cups) with no trace of yolk
2 t cream of tartar
Pinch of salt
5 cups granulated sugar
5 t vanilla

3 cups whipping cream
1/2 cup sugar
1/4 cup kirsch

Summer fruits, e.g., raspberries, cherries, kiwi, blueberries

Unless you have a very large mixer available, divide the meringue ingredients into several batches. Using a mixer, beat the whites in a metal (preferably copper) bowl until soft peaks start to form. Add salt and cream of tartar and then beat in two thirds of the sugar. Don't stop until the meringue is smooth, glossy and very firm. Stir in the vanilla and fold in the remaining sugar with a large rubber spatula. Using a pastry bag, pipe onto baking sheets lined with parchment paper. Make 3" circles of meringue, and then pipe a ring around the edge to form a basket. Bake at 225° for about 2 hours, until the meringues are firm and dry enough to pick up easily.

Whip the cream till firm and add the sugar and kirsch. Fill this into the cooled meringues and top with summer fruits.

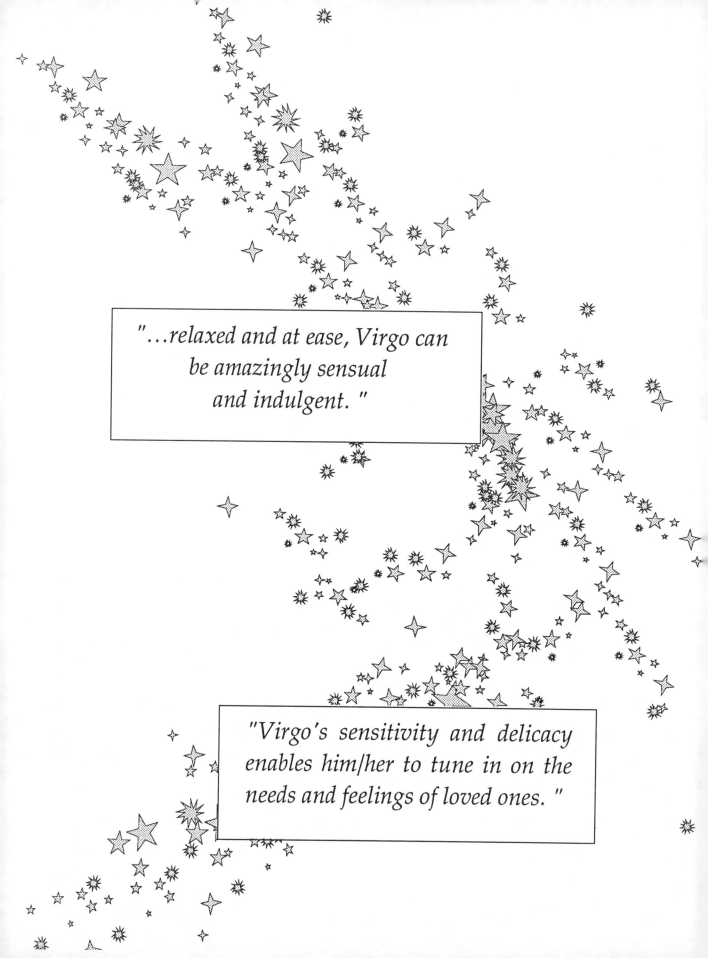

"...relaxed and at ease, Virgo can
be amazingly sensual
and indulgent."

"Virgo's sensitivity and delicacy
enables him/her to tune in on the
needs and feelings of loved ones."

VIRGO
The Perfect Dinner Party for 6

Kir
Smoked Salmon and Caviar Tart

Escalope of Veal with Green Peppercorns
Brown Rice
Spinach Creams
Hot Buttered Dinner Rolls

Pecan Roulade
Sauce Framboise

VIRGO

August 23-September 22

There's a cosmic joke making the rounds. What sign always neatly hangs up his/her clothes before making love? Yes, of course, it's Virgo. And yes again—it's true.

But it isn't true that anyone born between August 23 and September 22 is prim, prissy, devoid of romantic interest or expertise. While never obvious, this sign is a past master/mistress at the subtle art of seduction. Cool, calculating Virgos can—if they choose—detach their feelings from their actions in a manner that would be impossible—if not incomprehensible—to others.

One of the all time great lovers of history, Charles II (the Merry Monarch) was a Virgo, as was the Sun King, Louis XIV. A strong feminist who believed that women should enjoy the sexual autonomy that men take for granted was Margaret Sanger, a Virgo who changed history by introducing birth control. A sister in spirit as well as sign was Victoria Woodhull, who ran for president in 1872 on a platform that included free love.

Today one has only to observe Sophia Loren, Sean Connery, Jacqueline Bisset and Raquel Welch to dispel the popular misconception that Virgos are the cosmic janitors forever emptying ashtrays at the grand feast of life.

Mercury rules intelligence and communication — *all* forms of communication and that includes touch. An earth sign metaphorically as well as astrologically, once relaxed and at ease, Virgo can be amazingly sensual and indulgent. There's also a warmth and humor not found in the other earth signs.   Though gentle and modest, the Mercury wit is always present. Virgo's throw away lines are too good to miss, yet so often are.

Invariably attractive, always well groomed (Virgos probably take more baths and showers than all other signs together) there's an endearing secret lurking behind the super cool facade. Virgo simply cannot say "no" to anything little and helpless. Don't you imagine that St. Francis was a Virgo? I'm sure of it.

The sign of the virgin is associated with the harvest, Mother Nature at her strongest and most selective, separating the wheat from the chaff. Intuition is the keynote here. Virgo's sensitivity and delicacy enables him/her to tune in on the needs and feelings of loved ones. Often there's a rare and beautiful communion that makes words unnecessary.   **But** that intuition can work in other ways as well. Never, never attempt to deceive a Virgo. The savviest of signs, Virgo *always* knows where it's at.

Be warned: it's not wise to fool Mother Nature.

VIRGO'S Absolutely Perfect Dinner Party

It simply isn't true that Virgos boil their toothbrushes at night or wear rubber gloves to mix meatloaf.

Probably the least understood of all the signs, Virgo is a true individualist with keen perceptions and a brilliant, intuitive mind. Once this sign has learned to master detail rather than allowing detail to master her/him, Virgo can shape destiny with more certainty than any other sign. Maybe that's why there are more of them listed in the American *Who's Who* than any other sign.

Unfortunately telling Virgo to stop fussing is as hopeless as suggesting that Gemini give up gossip or Scorpio abandon amour.

Look into a Virgo home and what do you see? Books, magazines, newspapers, potted plants and a miniature drugstore. What do you smell? Bread baking, flowers from the garden and disinfectant. Here is a bastion of comfort, a place of learning and a refuge. Virgo's fragile nerves need plenty of play, affection, rest and contact with nature.

The most discriminating of all the signs, this innate selectivity is clearly reflected in the Virgo choice of lifestyle.

The saying, "If it's worth doing, it's worth doing right," was undoubtedly coined by a Virgo; but you can be certain this gathering will be much more than right. It'll be the top of the line in every sense. Quiet, gentle, possessed of a whimsical sense of humor and a genuine desire to please, Virgo enjoys displaying his/her competence.

Ms./Mr. Clean is nothing if not meticulous. The elegant, well appointed room will sparkle. The guest list will be small and well considered. As always with Virgo, the accent is on quality and not quanitity. And be certain the table conversation will sparkle too.

Virgos have as little patience with mental sloppiness as they have with dirt or vulgarity.

Crystal, silver and china will be exquisite—but practical. The flower arrangement, a harvest of late summer blooms, will be placed in such a way as to never obstruct the flow of conversation or the passing of food.

And as for the food. . .what can I say? Virgo plans and plans and plans. Preparations are well considered and then followed to the letter. This is the sign that knows how and does it so well.

Mercury, the magical magician of the cosmos, has created a fascinating paradox. Virgo can be deadly practical and divinely romantic all at one time. There's the ethereal ideal and the earthly wherewithal to make it fly. What can you expect?

Just perfection.

VIRGO — The Perfect Dinner Party for 6

♍ ♍ ♍ ♍ ♍ ♍ ♍ ♍ ♍ ♍ ♍ ♍ ♍ ♍

Kir
Smoked Salmon and Caviar Tart

Escalope of Veal with Green Peppercorns
Brown Rice
Spinach Creams
Hot Buttered Dinner Rolls

Pecan Roulade
Sauce Framboise

♍ ♍ ♍ ♍ ♍ ♍ ♍ ♍ ♍ ♍ ♍ ♍ ♍ ♍

Virgo Party Plan

The day before or morning of the party:

Prepare the tart pastry, filling and toppings, but do not assemble
Cook rice ready to reheat
Make dessert and sauce

Before the party:

Assemble the tart
Prepare the veal dish
Make spinach creams
Butter rolls and wrap for reheating
Garnish the dessert

During the party:

Serve the kirs
Reheat all main course dishes

♍ ♍ ♍ Kir ♍ ♍ ♍

Pour a glass of chilled white wine onto a teaspoon of Creme de Cassis in a wine glass and finish with a lemon twist.

♍ ♍ ♍ Smoked Salmon and Caviar Tart ♍ ♍ ♍

Crust:
   1 1/2 cups flour
   6 T butter
   pinch salt
   grated rind of 1 lemon
   1 egg beaten with a little lemon juice

Filling:
   8 oz cream cheese
   1/2 cup sour cream
   1 very finely chopped shallot
   Salt, pepper, Worcestershire sauce and
   tabasco to taste
   1/2 packet of gelatine

Toppings:
   8 oz neatly shredded smoked salmon
   2 oz caviar (red or black)
   Chopped white and finely sieved yolk of 1
   hard-boiled egg
   Very thinly sliced green onions

Variations on toppings:
   Chopped pimento, sliced black olives, sliced
   ham, shrimp, capers, etc.

Mix the flour, salt, butter and lemon rind and rub together until crumbly. Add the egg and lemon juice and mix together to form a soft dough. Work this into a 9" fluted pan with a removable bottom. Support the sides with strips of foil, prick the bottom with a fork and bake in a 350° oven for about 10-15 minutes, until lightly brown.

Mix the cream cheese, sour cream and seasonings together untl completely smooth. Add shallot. Sprinkle the gelatine over a very little cold water in a small pan, and when "sponged" dissolve it over gentle heat. Blend into the filling, and spread into the cooled pastry case.

Arrange the toppings of your choice in very neat circles, starting from the outside. Chill until serving time.

♍ ♍ ♍ *Escalope of Veal with Green Peppercorns* ♍ ♍ ♍

2 lbs pounded escalope of veal (or thinly sliced veal chops)
Flour seasoned with salt and pepper
Butter for frying
4 shallots, finely chopped
Garlic to taste
2 teaspoons flour
2 cups beef or veal stock
Juice of 1/2 orange
2 T green peppercorns
1 T Dijon mustard
1/2 cup white wine or 1/4 cup sherry
Sliced mushrooms (optional)
1/2 cup cream, to finish sauce
2 oranges and watercress to garnish

Coat the veal in seasoned flour and sear quickly on each side in hot butter. Remove the meat and juices from the pan. In a little extra butter, sauté the shallots and garlic, and when browning add the flour and cook for a couple of minutes. Blend in the stock, juice, peppercorns, mustard, wine and mushrooms and simmer the sauce, allowing it to reduce in volume and concentrate the flavors. Meanwhile, make julienne strips of orange peel and drop them into a pan of boiling water for a minute. Drain them and rinse under cold water.

When ready to serve, fry the slices of orange in a little butter and sugar to barely caramelize them. Finish the sauce with cream and salt and pepper to taste. Return the veal to the hot sauce and heat through for about 5 minutes (5 minutes longer for chops). Serve on a heated platter decorated with orange slices and watercress, and sprinkle julienne strips over the veal.

♍ ♍ ♍ *Brown Rice* ♍ ♍ ♍

Cook the rice according to instructions and store in a well-buttered, covered, oven-proof dish. Moisten with about 1/2 cup stock and reheat in an oven or microwave oven.

♍ ♍ ♍ *Spinach Creams* ♍ ♍ ♍

2 bunches fresh spinach
1-2 T butter
3/4 cup milk
Slice of onion, bayleaf and sprig of parsley
3 T butter
3 T flour
2 eggs
Salt, pepper and a grate of nutmeg

Butter 12 two inch muffin molds. Choose the largest spinach leaves and dip them by the stalks into boiling water for a few seconds. Line these into the molds with the upper sides of the leaves down in the molds. Use two or more leaves if necessary for each mold, to allow enough to cover over the tops. Break off the stalks.

Heat the onion, bayleaf and parsley gently with the milk. Cook the remaining spinach very briefly in a little salted boiling water, then drain and chop it finely. Melt the butter, stir in the flour and strain the hot milk into this. Whisk it over heat to give a thickened sauce. To this, add the spinach, eggs and seasonings. Spoon the mixture into lined cups, and cover the tops with the pieces of leaves hanging over the sides.

Before serving, cook the molds, sitting in a water bath, in a 350° oven for 20 minutes, until set. Turn out onto a platter.

♍ ♍ ♍ *Hot Buttered Dinner Rolls* ♍ ♍ ♍

Choose fresh buttery rolls or brioches, and almost split them in two. Spread with butter and wrap in foil for oven heating without drying. Heat at about 325° for 10 minutes.

♍ ♍ ♍ *Pecan Roulade with Sauce Framboise* ♍ ♍ ♍

Soufflé:
    6 egg whites
    6 egg yolks
    3/4 cup sugar
    1 T baking powder
    1 1/2 cups finely chopped pecans

Filling:
    1 cup whipping cream
    1/4 cup powdered sugar
    1 teaspoon vanilla
    1 T kirsch
    1 cup fresh or frozen and drained raspberries

Sauce Framboise:
    1 cup fresh or frozen raspberries
    Extra sugar for fresh berries
    Few tablespoons kirsch to taste

Garnish:
Whipped cream rosettes topped with raspberries and pecan halves.

With an electric mixer, whisk the yolks and sugar until they are thick and lightly colored. Whip the egg whites in a metal bowl — preferably copper — until they are in firm peaks. Add the pecans and baking powder to the yolk mixture, and gently fold in the egg whites. Line a cookie sheet with parchment paper, grease it well, and spread the soufflé mixture evenly on top. Bake for 20 minutes in a preheated 350° oven till puffed and set. Cool slightly, and roll it up around another piece of parchment paper, peeling the cooking paper off the back.

Whip the cream until firm and flavor with the sugar, vanilla and kirsch. When the roulade is cold, carefully unroll it and spread with the cream. Lay on the raspberries and roll up again. Sprinkle the top with powdered sugar. Puree the sauce ingredients until smooth. Garnish the roulade and chill for serving.

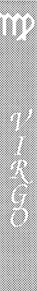

"Of all the planets, Libra's children want most to please and do it so well…"

"Affection, sympathy and charm are balanced by an astute mind and the wit to use it. "

LIBRA
A Romantic Dinner For Two

Raw Oysters on the Half Shell

Roast Game Hen with Cherries and Red Wine Sauce
Wild and Brown Rice
Tomatoes Stuffed with Pine Nuts and Parsley

Flaming Crepes Suzettes

LIBRA

September 23-October 22

Does it come as any surprise to hear that your radiant ruler is Venus, planetary symbol of attraction? The whole world adores you.

Late night TV reveals your astral siblings at the height of their appeal. Could anyone resist Charles Boyer, Brigitte Bardot, Rita Hayworth or Marcello Mastroianni? Would anyone care to?

Amour comes to you so easily (and sometimes so often) that your tender heart may be taxed trying to reconcile yesterday's holdovers with today's Grand Passion—not to mention the alluring possibilities of tomorrow.

Of all the planets, Libra's children want most to please and do it so well—not a simple task with so many attractive prospects about. Is it any surprise that yours is the sign of love *and* litigation?

Since Libras have so much trouble making up their minds, it's easy to become involved with aspects and fragments of many people—spending years yearning for the missing pieces. Ah, such romantics …and what heart breakers!

Though your views may change like a sudden breeze—after all, you *are* an air sign—you have the quality of inspiring the very best in those about you. Affection, sympathy and charm are balanced by an astute mind and the wit to use it. The peacemaker of the cosmos, you understand the true benefits of sharing and harmony and can impart them easily to others.

Yes, you may, upon occasion, fall in love with love. The results may be disillusioning, but fragments of the romance will linger on and on and on. Rest assured, you'll never be forgotten—nor will you forget. Momentary pique will fade—who can remain angry with Libra?—leaving in its place a secret cache of bittersweet memories. Sleepless nights will find you counting past loves as other signs count sheep. Don't tell Minerva you never tried it!

Libra's Love Feast

How does it feel to be the darling of the cosmos? Most of the other signs would love to have your problems.

Problems? Yes, there are a few. Sympathetic, affectionate and gentle, you have a hard time saying "no." *And* those extraordinary good looks attract all sorts of opportunities and temptations. So much for problems. Birthdays are for pleasure and pleasuring.

You were made for parties and parties for you. Your phone rings off the hook with invitations of all kinds, but you prefer small, intimate gatherings. The crush of large crowds can upset your natural sense of harmony.

A past mistress/master of the delicacies, nuances and sentiments of romance, you're at your very best in one-to-one situations. What could be more appropriate than an intimate dinner for two?

Your home environment is already perfect—an elegant blending of imagination and artistry. Add to this a shining damask tablecloth (pink, of course), gleaming silver, sparkling crystal, and the centerpiece, a single perfect rose rising from an exquisite bud vase.

Naturally background music is a must. Consider the works of those true to form Libran composers: Franz Liszt, George Gerswhin and John Lennon. John Lennon? Have you forgotten "I Want to Hold Your Hand"? The lovebeat is definitely there as well as the sentiment.

air sign

LIBRA — A Romantic Dinner for 2

♎ ♎ ♎ ♎ ♎ ♎ ♎ ♎ ♎ ♎ ♎ ♎ ♎ ♎

Raw Oysters on the Half Shell

Roast Game Hen with Cherries and Red Wine Sauce
Wild and Brown Rice
Tomatoes Stuffed with Pine Nuts and Parsley

Flaming Crepes Suzettes

♎ ♎ ♎ ♎ ♎ ♎ ♎ ♎ ♎ ♎ ♎ ♎ ♎ ♎

Libra Party Plan

The day before or earlier in the day of the party:

Prepare spicy mayonnaise
Stuff the tomatoes
Make and fill the crepes

Prepare the game hens for roasting and start the sauce

Before the party:

Arrange the oysters
Cook the rice

During the party:

Finish the game hens and sauce
Heat tomatoes and rice
Heat and flame crepes

⌁⌁⌁ *Raw Oysters on the Half Shell* ⌁⌁⌁

12 very fresh oysters
Lemon juice
Tabasco

Clean and shuck the oysters. Place them on the half shells, sprinkle with a little lemon juice and arrange them on a bed of crushed ice. Serve with hot sauce on the side, or with a little spicy mayonnaise.

⌁⌁⌁ *Spicy Mayonnaise* ⌁⌁⌁

2 egg yolks
Pinch salt, white pepper and dry mustard
1 cup vegetable oil
1 T each lemon juice and white wine vinegar
1 T dijon mustard
1 t horseradish
Dash of tomato paste for color

Place the yolks, salt, pepper and mustard in a blender, and very slowly, with the blender running, drip in the oil. Gradually increase the stream as the mayonnaise thickens. Blend in the other ingredients and chill well.

Roast Game Hen with Cherries and Red Wine Sauce

2 game hens
2 T butter
1/2 onion
1 stick celery
1 carrot
2 T olive oil
1 T flour
1 cup beef stock
1/2 cup red wine
1 bay leaf
1 crushed clove garlic
1 t tomato paste
1 T dijon mustard
1 T red currant jelly
Salt and pepper to taste
6 oz fresh or canned pitted cherries

Season the game hen cavities with pepper and fry quickly in hot butter until the skin is golden brown. Place them in a small roasting dish and set aside.

Finely dice the onion, celery and carrot and fry in oil. When tender, add the flour and continue to cook, scraping the pan when necessary, until the contents of the pan turn a dark russet brown. (This takes time but makes for a rich dark sauce.) Blend in stock, wine, bay leaf, salt, pepper, garlic and tomato paste. Simmer the sauce for about 20 minutes. You can work ahead up to this point.

Meanwhile, precook the wild rice and place in a covered serving dish with 1 T butter and 1 T sherry.

30 minutes before sitting down for the oyster course, place game hens and rice in a preheated 375° oven and cook for about 45 minutes. Add the mustard, jelly and cherries to the sauce, plus the quail drippings, and season to taste. Reheat the rice.

To serve, mound the hot rice on a warmed serving platter, arrange the game hens on top and spoon over a little sauce. Top with cherries and serve the remaining sauce separately.

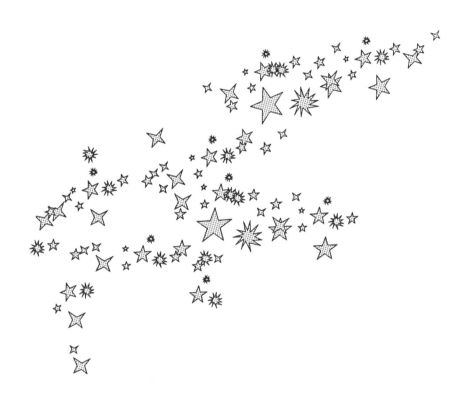

2 ripe tomatoes
Salt and pepper to taste
3 T butter
1/2 cup pine nuts
1/4 cup finely chopped parsley
1 crushed clove garlic
1/2 cup chopped spinach

Cut the tomatoes in half and scoop out the insides. Sprinkle with a little salt and drain them upside down. Meanwhile, sauté the pine nuts in butter until golden brown. Add the garlic, parsley, spinach and seasonings and cook for 5 minutes. Spoon into the tomato halves and arrange them in a heatproof dish.

Twenty minutes before serving, place them in a pre-heated 350° oven, or place in a microwave oven on high for about 4 minutes, or until heated through.

2 beaten eggs

1/3 cup milk

1/3 cup water

3/4 cup flour

1 T melted butter

2 T sugar

1 t vanilla

Grated rind of 1 orange

Orange Butter:

4 T butter

1 orange

1 T sugar

2 T Grand Marnier

1/2 cup brandy

Add the liquids to the beaten eggs in a bowl and gradually whisk in the flour until smooth. Add all other batter ingredients, beat well and allow to rest for at least 30 minutes. (This prevents the crepes from developing a rubbery texture.) Adjust the consistency of the batter if necessary. Cook paper thin crepes in a minimal amount of butter in a crepe pan. Select 3 perfect crepes for each of you, and stack, wrap and freeze the rest.

Combine the butter, grated orange rind, sugar, Grand Marnier and a tablespoon of the orange juice. Don't be concerned if the mixture is not smooth. Spread the butter between the crepes, fold in half and then half again to form triangles. Place them overlapping in a heat-proof dish and set aside.

Heat crepes for about 10 minutes in a preheated 375° oven. (They do not work in a microwave.) Gently warm the brandy in a small pan. Extinguish the lights and flame the heated brandy as you pour it over the crepes at the table.

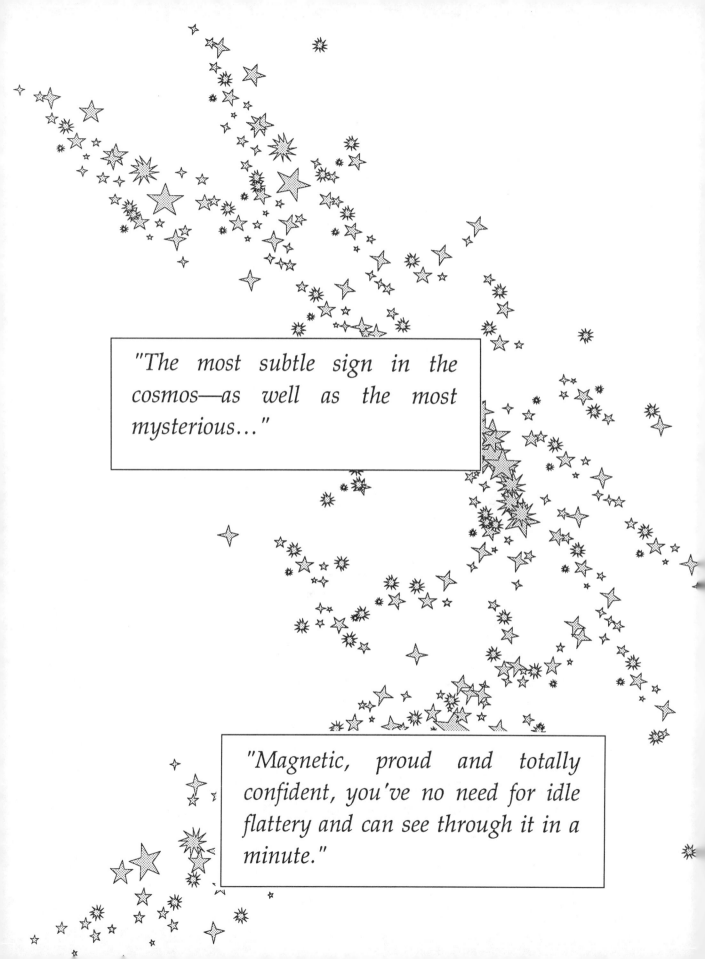

"The most subtle sign in the cosmos—as well as the most mysterious..."

"Magnetic, proud and totally confident, you've no need for idle flattery and can see through it in a minute."

SCORPIO
A Witchy Affair for 25

Black Velvets
Steak Tartare
Pumpkin Soup in a Pumpkin

Transylvanian Lamb
Herbed Noodles
Glazed Parsleyed Carrots

Chocolate Orange Mousse Torte

SCORPIO

October 23 - November 22

No one really understands you, do they? Yet so many *think* they do. What invariably happens when someone learns your sign? They either back off, suddenly frightened, or become very interested in what you're doing later in the evening.

Whether the reaction is fear or leer, you don't like it.   Secrets are a Scorpio's private passion. The most subtle sign in the cosmos—as well as the most mysterious—you like nothing better than to probe into dark corners to discover what others are up to, yet you regard your own feelings and affairs as strictly off limits. What alarms some is the uncanny gift you Scorps have of perceiving exactly what other people don't wish to have known—often before they're aware of it themselves.

The obvious lure of the Scorpio is the much talked about sexuality. What most don't realize is that Scorpio is every bit as selective as Virgo when it comes to love or friendship.   Of the three water signs, yours is frozen fire and it doesn't thaw easily.

Magnetic, proud and totally confident, you've no need for idle flattery and can see through it in a minute.   Penetratingly analytical and intuitive, you know almost immediately when you've met the "right" one. Not only can you recognize a future lover at first glance, you can transfer this perception to him/her.   Now isn't that some kind of magic?

All astrologers have something scintillating to say about Scorpios.

Linda Goodman (*Sun Signs*) described them most aptly when she wrote, "Brimming over inside with passion though it's kept under control by a poised, frosty attitude toward strangers and a surface smoothness suggestive of black velvet."

Does that remind you of anyone?   Sure it does, all those Grace Kelly films resurfacing on the late, late show.   Well, of course, the glamorous Princess Grace of Monaco was a Scorpio.   Not to mention Katherine Hepburn, Gene Tierney and Vivien Leigh.

Do you know before the phone rings just who's calling?   Do your dreams literally come true?   Is talking to your plants as natural as watering them? Yes! Yes! Yes! What else is new? You're a Scorpio. As such you see nothing far out about ESP, life after death (or before birth), karma—all that weird stuff that's just beginning to intrigue other signs.

With Mars marshalling a sheer force of energy and animal instinct and Pluto spearheading the regeneration of the primitive self into the divine, yours is the most powerful of the twelve signs. In other words, Mars works at a gut level making you the past master/mistress of the hunch while Pluto is the cosmic link with infinity, the mysteries of the universe.

You always know at the deepest level what the result of your choices will be regardless of surfaces appearances.   You see the pretense and superficiality and aren't fooled by them—even in yourself.

water sign

SCORPIO — That Old Black Magic
— A Witchy Affair For 25

When it comes to party time, guests will feel a sense of excitement knowing that anything can happen and probably will. The only thing one can be certain of is warmth and intimacy. Behind the black velvet poise there's a haunting sweetness about Scorpio that invites loyalty, and this is very much a two-way proposition. For Scorpio, friendship is no sometime thing; relationships are forever.

A sign that adores sensuality every bit as much as Taurus, the Scorpio home will be well appointed. Expect thick rugs, low comfy couches and silken cushions, but there will be other touches as well—a jungle of plants, masks, amulets, talisman garnered from native bazaars and garage sales. Scorpio is nothing if not eclectic.

Since Scorpio can and does do anything he/she really wants to do, the party will be well planned and those plans carefully carried out. Guests will be expertly wined and dined. You can count on that, but that's all you can count on. Expect only the unexpected.

The witch that lurks behind every Scorpio is certain to come out of the broom closet to celebrate a natal day that comes appropriately close to Halloween. A sign that adores the night (ideally dark and stormy) and never saw a monster movie she/he didn't like might very well plan a costume party. . ."Vampira, meet the Hunchback of Notre Dame." "Dr. Frankenstein, do try the steak tartar. That handsome werewolf over there prepared it himself."

A seance is another possibility, or tarot readings. At the very least a Ouija board will be at the ready. What does it spell? W-E-I-R-D W-I-L-D W-O-N-D-E-R-F-U-L.

It'll be a night to remember.

SCORPIO – A Witchy Affair for 25

♏ ♏ ♏ ♏ ♏ ♏ ♏ ♏ ♏ ♏ ♏ ♏ ♏ ♏ ♏

Black Velvets
Steak Tartare
Pumpkin Soup in a Pumpkin

Transylvanian Lamb
Herbed Noodles
Glazed Parsleyed Carrots

Chocolate Orange Mousse Torte

♏ ♏ ♏ ♏ ♏ ♏ ♏ ♏ ♏ ♏ ♏ ♏ ♏ ♏ ♏

Scorpio Party Plan

The day before:
Carve the pumpkin
Make the soup
Make the lamb casserole
Make the tortes

Before the party:
Assemble and arrange the steak tartare
Pick and arrange fall leaves to garnish the pumpkin
Steam the carrots and mix the glaze ingredients
Cook noodles and chop herbs
Garnish the torte

During the party:
Mix black velvets
Heat soup, lamb and carrots
Toss the noodles

♏ SCORPIO

ꟽ ꟽ ꟽ   *Black Velvets* ꟽ ꟽ ꟽ

Mix equal amounts of chilled champagne and stout in champagne glasses.

ꟽ ꟽ ꟽ   *Steak Tartare* ꟽ ꟽ ꟽ

2 lbs freshly ground raw sirloin
Salt and black pepper to taste
1 T dijon mustard
2 egg yolks
4 T olive oil
2 T white wine vinegar
3 finely chopped shallots
2 cloves crushed garlic
1/2 cup finely chopped parsley
Small bottle capers
1/2 small can mashed anchovies

Garnish:
2 hard boiled eggs
Anchovy fillets
Finely chopped green onions
Capers

Thoroughly combine the meat with all of the seasonings, reserving half the capers for garnish. Form into a mound and decorate with small piles of chopped egg whites, sieved egg yolks, onions and capers. Serve with cocktail rye bread, pumpernickel, or with crackers.

♏ ♏ ♏   *Pumpkin Soup in a Pumpkin* ♏ ♏ ♏

    1 large pumpkin for carving
    4 oz butter
    3 large onions, chopped finely
    1 1/2 cups green onions, sliced
    1 1/2 lb small mushrooms, sliced neatly
    2 16-oz cans pumpkin puree (not sweetened)
    8-10 cups chicken stock
    Bay leaf, salt and pepper, grated nutmeg
    1 t sugar
    2 T Worcestershire sauce
    4 cups half and half

Choose an attractive pumpkin that stands up easily and remove the cap with a zig-zag cutting motion. Hollow out the seeds and membranes and scrape clean. Rinse with boiling water. In a large pan, saute the onions in butter until limp and then add the mushrooms. Cook for 5 minutes and then add pumpkin, stock and seasonings. Simmer for about 30 minutes, cool slightly and stir in the half and half. Work ahead to this point.

Heat the pumpkin in a 300° oven for about 15 minutes. Reheat the soup, either on the stove or in a microwave oven, and adjust the seasonings to taste. Pour the soup into the pumpkin, replace the cap, and garnish it with fall colored leaves. It will remain hot for some time. Expect surprised guests when the centerpiece becomes the first course.

♏ ♏ ♏   *Herbed Noodles* ♏ ♏ ♏

Cook pasta or noodles of your choice al dente in plenty of simmering salted water, and then drain. If preparing them ahead, turn into a large pan of lukewarm water to prevent sticking. Before serving, toss in a little olive oil and butter, season with garlic, salt and pepper, and a generous handful of chopped fresh herbs, e.g., chives, parsley, tarragon.

♏ ♏ ♏ *Glazed Parsleyed Carrots* ♏ ♏ ♏

5 lbs sweet carrots, preferably small
4 oz butter
Juice of 2 oranges
Julienne strips of peel from 2 oranges
2 T brown sugar
1 T ground ginger
Pinch of salt
1/2 cup chopped parsley

Peel the carrots, and leave them whole if small, or cut into diagonal slices. Steam them until barely tender. Mix all the glaze ingredients together and before serving, heat the carrots in a large pan with the glaze until they are hot and shiny.

♏ ♏ ♏ *Chocolate Orange Mousse Torte* ♏ ♏ ♏

Crust:

6 cups chocolate wafer crumbs
6 oz ground toasted nuts (e.g., hazelnuts or almonds)
4 T finely grated orange rind
1 cup melted butter
orange juice to moisten if necessary

Mousse:

1 lb semisweet chocolate
1/2 lb unsweetened chocolate
8 egg yolks
1 cup cocoa powder
grated rind of 2 oranges
About 20 dried apricots, finely chopped
4 T Grand Marnier or other orange liqueur
4 cups whipping cream

1/2 cup powdered sugar

8 egg whites

2 T sugar

Grand Marnier Cream Layer (optional):

1 cup whipping cream

4 T powdered sugar

4 T Grand Marnier

Chocolate Leaves:

4 oz chocolate

Camellia leaves

Garnish:

Julienne strips of orange rind, blanched in boiling water for 1 minute

For the crust, grind the wafers, nuts and orange rind together, moisten with the melted butter and juice if necessary and press onto the sides and bottom of 2 10" springform pans. Chill while assembling the mousse. Melt the chocolates in a double boiler or microwave, taking care not to overheat and burn the chocolate. Blend in the yolks, cocoa, orange rind, apricots and Grand Marnier. Whip the cream with the sugar until stiff and beat in the 2 T of sugar. Fold the chocolate mixture, cream and whites together gently, and turn out into the crusts. Chill well to set.

Whip up the Grand Marnier cream ingredients until firm and spread carefully over the top of the chilled tortes.

Melt the chocolate for the leaves, and spread onto the greased backs of firm camellia leaves. Freeze these, and gently peel off the leaves when set.

Use the chocolate leaves and julienne strips of orange as a garnish when the tortes are removed from the pans. Keep cold till serving time.

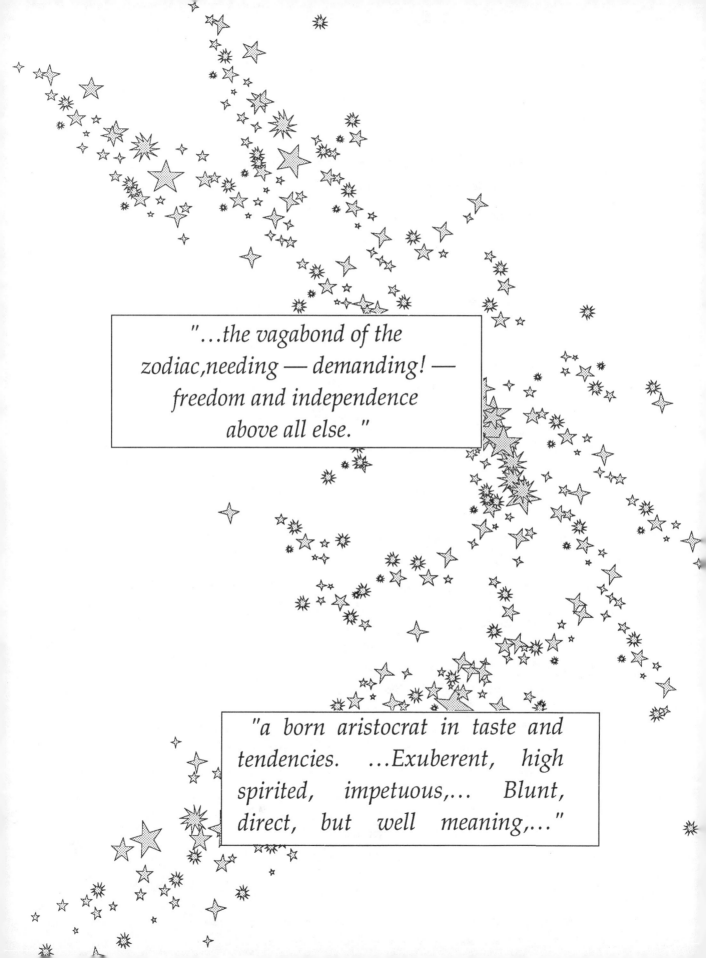

"...the vagabond of the zodiac, needing — demanding! — freedom and independence above all else. "

"a born aristocrat in taste and tendencies. ...Exuberent, high spirited, impetuous,... Blunt, direct, but well meaning,..."

SAGITTARIUS
A Tailgate Party
For 16 Super Souls

Hot Mulled Wine
Pepperoni and Bean Soup

Smoked Salmon Quiche
Crunchy Celery Salad with Lemon Cream Dressing
Mushrooms à la Greque

Cranberry Walnut Bread
The Ultimate Chocolate Chip Cookie

SAGITTARIUS

November 23-December 21

The most free-spirited and volatile of the fire signs, you're the vagabond of the zodiac, needing — demanding! — freedom and independence above all else. The Don Juan (or Juana) of the cosmos, your love of risk taking, romance and adventure is only tempered by your idealism and sincere desire to help.

Like the man from La Mancha, yours is often the impossible dream for you're always seeking the perfect mate, the perfect job, the perfect home. This fast paced approach to life may lead down some strange byways, but one thing's certain, they will always be exciting. Would the sign that spends most of its life in the fast lane have it any other way?

You literally thrive on hair breath escapes and that includes personal entanglements. Much as you adore conquest and companionship, you abhor restrictions. The bright side to this (from the other person's point of view) is that you're rarely possessive. So concerned are you with your own freedom and independence, that you're quite magnanimous about granting the same rights to others. Where careers and/or creativity are concerned, you're more than willing to allow a lover to do his/her own thing. Rarely —if ever—are you threatened by the accomplishments that invariably result from all that free time. You even brag about them.

Actually, you're seldom found with a love that doesn't already have some accomplishments. You need a partner with wit and brilliance to match your own. Moody, deliberate, slow-moving people are anathema to you. You'll never understand them or they you.

A complex character who is more apt to know what you don't want than what you do, you can cause a lot of trouble—but have such fun doing it! You're a sign that loves action, the outdoors and travel, but can adapt to any surroundings—since you rarely stay anywhere for long.

The child of Jupiter, it's only natural that you're a born aristocrat in taste and tendencies. An instinctive flirt, your innate desire to expand can overpower your sense of loyalty. Just recall Jupiter's extensive and varied love life! A proud, dynamic planet, Jupiter has much physical and mental energy that must be discharged. The tendency is to overdo, going to extremes whether it be eating too much, drinking too much or trying to experience and understand *everything*.

Exuberant, high spirited, impetuous, Jupiter has little—if any patience with restrictions. Witness all those thunderbolts! The Sagittarian temper is well known. Surely this is the sign of Donald Duck. Blunt, direct, but well meaning, Donald's rages are instantaneous, incendiary and raucous but short-lived. He's never petty, never a grudge holder. How could he be? His attention span doesn't allow for it.

More traditionally, Sagittarius is symbolized by the centaur, that mysterious, mythic creature, half human, half horse, his bow forever raised. The centaur shoots many arrows high into the air, then gallops off in all directions in pursuit of her/his grand design. What matters most is the excitement of the aim, the fascination of the pursuit, the experience of the journey.

Some arrows are lost forever, but isn't that better than aiming too low?

fire sign

SAGITTARIUS — a Tailgate Party For 16 Super Souls

One would rarely describe Sagittarius as a domestic delight. Neither male nor female finds the thought of sinks, stoves and diapers very intriguing.

The cry of the archer is Freedom! Sports, travel and crusades are physical expressions of the urge to pursue the grand adventure beckoning at the edge of the horizon. Sagittarians are often prophets of a new order. At the very least they bring fresh insights to the old.

Famous crusaders in the fields of writing, music, theater and art were Mark Twain, Maria Callas, Noel Coward and Toulouse Lautrec. Another Sagittarian, Gustave Flaubert, revolutionized literature by breaking free from the moral strictures of his time. As good an example of the centaur freedom song as Beethoven's Fifth Symphony (a WWII rallying symbol) is Frank Sinatra singing "My Way."

When channeled that crackling energy will invariably illuminate some aspect of the human condition. Consider Disraeli, Churchill or more contemporarily, Jane Fonda. Look for controversy and one can generally find a Sagittarian centered there.

They're equally lively at play. This is the sign that adores good food, fine wines, fast cars, private planes, expensive clothes, Gambling, if not in a casino, then in the stockmarket is a passion. Sagittarians also play their hunches in land speculation or in the business world. Fortunately Jupiter, the planet of luck and largess, looks after his own. Never is a Sagittarian born without a gift and the wit to use it.

If there's one adjective to encompass all Sagittarians its "trendy." This sign is the first to spot the future best seller, the rising star, the up and coming columnist, the latest consciousness raising device, the soon to be discovered restaurant, bar or disco. In any circle, trust a Sagittarian to know what's about to be "IN." Fluid, flexible, high rolling Sagittarians are always where the action is.

They've also got a penchant for making contacts. As gregarious as a Gemini, but even more quixotic, Sagittarius is the quintessential party animal.

Since home is most certainly not where the heart is, the Sagittarian party is apt to be a prelude to something else. The sign that's forgotten the past, moves through the present with the future clearly in sight, Saj can't or won't sit or stand still very long.

Tailormade to his/her taste is the tailgate party before a sporting event. The guest list will be varied. Sagittarians are marvelous mixers. Mental status seekers, they seek out the movers and shakers of the world for playmates. No one is ever bored at a Sagittarian soirée. Highly creative, exuberant and optimistic, he/she seeks and finds the same kind of high-keyed individuals. No embarrassing pauses or lagging conversations.

Jupiter, the lord of the planets, expects and receives the very best, so guests can be assured of fine food and wine. Like Sagittarius, the food will be spicy, a bit different—something of a conversation piece. The outdoor atmosphere, the impetus of the upcoming game, the break from tradition and routine promises flash, dash, panache.

But then, Jumping Jupiter! What else would one expect from a Sagittarian?

SAGITTARIUS — A Tailgate Party for 16

Hot Mulled Wine
Pepperoni and Bean Soup

Smoked Salmon Quiche
Crunchy Celery Salad with Lemon Cream Dressing
Mushrooms à la Greque

Cranberry Walnut Bread
The Ultimate Chocolate Chip Cookie

Sagittarius Party Plan

The day before:

    Make the soup
    Make the quiches
    Make the mushrooms à la Greque
    Bake the bread
    Mix the cookie dough

Before the game:

    Assemble the celery salad
    Bake the cookies
    Slice the bread
    Heat the soup and place in thermos
    Heat mulled wine and place in thermos
    Pack the hamper

At the game:

    Unpack and eat

↗ ↗ ↗ Hot Mulled Wine ↗ ↗ ↗

1 magnum red wine

1 magnum white or rosé wine

1 cup rum

Honey or sugar to taste

1 lemon and 1 orange liberally stuck with whole cloves

Orange and lemon slices to float in the punch

2 T cinnamon

1 t allspice

Cinnamon sticks to stir each drink

Heat the ingredients together until hot but not boiling. Serve hot with the fruit slices and cinnamon sticks.

⤴ ⤴ ⤴ *Pepperoni and Bean Soup* ⤴ ⤴ ⤴

1/2 lb lean bacon

3 onions, chopped

3 crushed cloves garlic

2 cups small white beans, soaked overnight in water

3 T flour

About 6 cups beef stock

1 cup chopped celery

1 cup diced tomatoes

3 T tomato paste

2 cups red wine

About 1 1/2 lbs pepperoni sausage

Salt and pepper to taste

2 bay leaves

1 t chopped thyme

Dice the bacon and fry until cooked but not crisp. Discard excess fat and add onions and garlic to the pan. Meanwhile, bring the beans to a boil in 4 cups water, then simmer, adding more water if necessary as they cook. When the onions start to brown, blend in the flour, cook for a minute or two and then blend in the stock. Bring to a boil and add vegetables and seasonings. Simmer for 30 minutes. When the beans are cooked, add them and their water, along with the wine and sausages and continue cooking the soup slowly.

Adjust the thickness of the soup by boiling it down or adding more water, and the seasonings if necessary. Serve very hot.

SAGITTARIUS

4 cups flour
Pinch salt
8 oz butter
1/2 cup Parmesan cheese
Few tablespoons ice water for mixing
1 lb cream cheese
4 eggs
1/2 cup parmesan cheese
1 lb smoked salmon
3 cups half and half
Juice of 1 lemon
Salt, pepper, and a generous pinch of nutmeg
1 lemon, very thinly sliced

Mix together the flour, salt, butter and cheese with a pastry cutter or in a food processor until well mixed and crumbly. Stir in just enough water to form a ball. Knead the dough lightly until smooth, and chill for half an hour or so before dividing into 2 and rolling out thinly. Line two 9" or 10" quiche pans. Bake "blind" for about 10 minutes in a 350° oven either by supporting the sides with strips of crumpled foil or by covering the bottom with waxed or parchment paper and beans or rice.

To make the filling, beat the cream cheese with the eggs until smooth and then add all other ingredients except lemon slices. Place these carefully around the top of the quiches when the filling has been poured into the half-cooked pastry shells. Bake at 350° until set and golden brown, about 30 minutes. Serve hot or cold.

SAGITTARIUS

1 large head of celery
1 cup fresh walnuts or pecans
4 crisp apples
1 cup cooked corn kernels
1/4 cup chopped green onions

Lemon cream dressing:
1/2 cup mayonnaise
1/2 cup plain yogurt
Grated rind and juice of 1 lemon
Salt and pepper
1 t caraway seeds

Mix dressing ingredients together. Chop the cleaned celery into small diagonal slivers. Chop the nuts coarsely and cut the apples into chunks. Mix all of the salad ingredients with the dresing and chill well. Serve mounded on lettuce leaves.

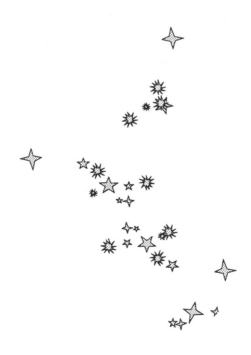

SAGITTARIUS

⚐ ⚐ ⚐ Mushrooms à la Greque ⚐ ⚐ ⚐

1 1/2 lbs mushrooms
1/2 lb small whole onions
Olive oil
Salt and pepper
Juice of 1 lemon
1 t thyme
Pinch of oregano
About 1/2 cup chopped fresh herbs, e.g., parsley, chives
1/2 cup tomato paste

Clean the onions, leaving them whole if small, or quartering them if they are larger, and blanch them for 1 minute in boiling water. Drain them, dry and saute in the olive oil. Meanwhile, clean the mushrooms, and when the onions are beginning to brown, add them, whole or quartered. Sauté over fairly high heat, adding a little more oil if necessary. Then add all of the seasonings and heat through for a few minutes. This dish may be served hot or cold.

SAGITTARIUS

✑ ✑ ✑ *Cranberry Walnut Bread* ✑ ✑ ✑

1 1/2 cups flour

1 t baking soda

1 t baking powder

Pinch salt

3/4 cup sugar

Grated rind of 2 oranges

4 oz butter

1 T lemon juice and juice of the 2 oranges

3 eggs

1 1/2 cups fresh cranberries

1 cup walnuts

Mix the flour, soda, baking powder and salt together. Cream the butter with the orange peel and sugar. Blend in the juices and the eggs. Fold in the cranberries and the nuts, then the flour mixture. Turn into a well-buttered loaf pan and bake at 350° until firm and browned, about 45 minutes. The mixture could also be baked in muffin cups.

4 oz butter
1/2 cup brown sugar
1/4 cup sugar
2 t vanilla
1 t almond extract
Pinch each of baking soda and baking powder
1 egg
1-2 T water
3/4 cup flour
Pinch salt
1/4 cup oats
1/4 cup shredded coconut
6-8 oz semi-sweet chocolate chips
1/2 cup chopped nuts
Grated rind and juice of 1 orange

Cream the butter, sugars and extracts until light and smooth. This can be conveniently done in a food processor. Blend in baking soda and baking powder, water and egg. Stir in the flour, salt, oats and coconut, and then add chips, nuts and orange rind and juice. Chill the dough.

Using an ice cream scoop or large spoon, mound balls of dough on a greased cookie sheet, and flatten them slightly. Bake at 350° for about 10 minutes. To keep them chewy, underbake them slightly; further cooking with crisp them more.

Due to dough tasting and sampling it will probably be necessary to make at least 2 batches for the tailgate party.

SAGITTARIUS

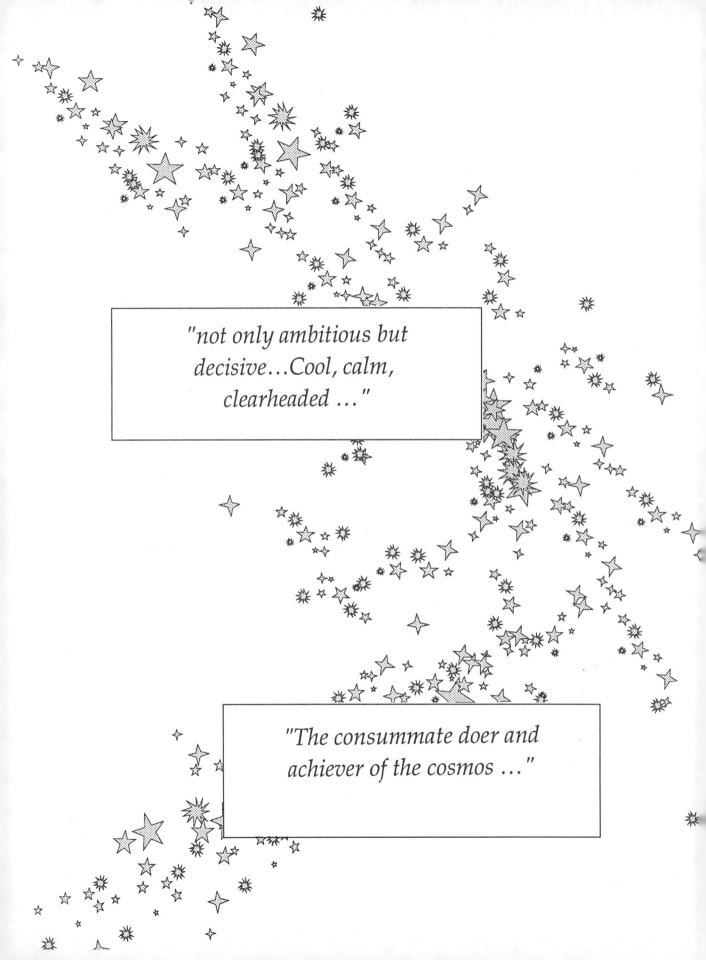

"not only ambitious but decisive...Cool, calm, clearheaded ..."

"The consummate doer and achiever of the cosmos ..."

CAPRICORN
An Elegant New Year's Eve Cocktail Party for 30 to 130

Martinis

Smoked Salmon and Dill Christmas Trees
Marscapone Torte
Prawn Christmas Tree
Baked Brie in Puff Pastry with Sliced Apples
Sesame Scallops
Mushroom Tarragon Pastries
Marinaded Lamb Skewers
Potato Skins with Sour Cream and Cheese

Brandied Mince Pies

CAPRICORN

December 22-January 19

The old saying "one step at a time" was undoubtedly invented by a Capricorn, for—more than any other sign—Caps see and understand the big picture.

One of the best ways to psyche out a sign is to check its position in the zodiac—the astral chart representing the sum total of human experiences. Note there's a logical progression from foolish Aries to world weary Pisces. Capricorn, as the tenth sign, stands guard over the tenth station of the zodiac—the sphere of power and achievement in the world of getting and spending. Of course there's a natural urge in almost everyone to prove oneself on the battleground of competition for the material things of this world; but—by virtue of the sign's astral heritage—that urge reaches its peak in Capricorn.

Saturn's children are not only ambitious but decisive. Very possibly the term "executive decision" was coined by a Cap. What this sign decides is not only right for now but serves some future purpose as well. Cool, calm, clearheaded Caps are always in demand when *someone* has got to decide.

The consummate doer and achiever of the cosmos, Capricorn is a natural "success" sign; but it's almost always a gradual success that evolves slowly. Remember Marlene Dietrich and Cary Grant weren't built in a day!

The Capricorn love scenario begins so quietly that one might not even notice. It's easy to mistake Capricorn's romantic interest as merely a desire for friendship and nothing more. Both sexes born under this sign are so discreet that it takes a Scorpio type to pick up even a clue that he or she might have something else in mind. But, given the achievement score of this sign, the success of the venture should be a foregone conclusion.

Capricorns often appear remote, even cool, but beneath that elegant facade lurks an earth sign with some lively and demanding proclivities. Romance with a Cap is like having dessert last—and isn't that where it belongs?

CAPRICORN

An Elegant New Year's Eve Cocktail Party for 30 to 130

Naturally a Capricorn soiree is going to be a real "power" affair. A sign that reveres tradition will insist upon the best of everything. If Caps don't inherit heirlooms, they slowly acquire someone else's at auctions, estate sales even garage sales—count on Capricorns to detect the real treasure that others overlook.

Born near the time of the winter solstice with roots reaching back to Saturnalia—the lusty ancestor of our New Year's Eve—Capricorn's solar return falls during the holiday season. What better time for a party?

The decor promises to be arresting. Crimson fading to shades of garnet with surprise touches of black. Many Caps will elect to wear black to their gala. Few signs are as aware of its seductive effect.

Contributing to the ambience one might hear background music, courtesy of other Capricorns: Joan Baez or Nat King Cole; Pablo Casals, Arthur Rubinstein or David Bowie.

Despite the impressive air of elegance, the atmosphere will be positively glowing. Caps are the late bloomers of the cosmos. The slogan, "You're not getting older, you're getting better" perfectly describes Saturn's darling who has the patience to appreciate life fully.

As for the party fare. . .what to expect? Just perfection. (The Capricorn "goat" scales social peaks as well as financial ones.) This will be the absolutely perfect cocktail party. The martinis will be icy. The champagne chilled and bubbly.

You Capricorns are the best of all possible planners. Believe it, practice it. Live it, enjoy it.

CAPRICORN –
An Elegant New Year's Eve Cocktail Party for 30 - 130

♑ ♑ ♑ ♑ ♑ ♑ ♑ ♑ ♑ ♑ ♑ ♑ ♑ ♑ ♑

Martinis

Smoked Salmon and Dill Christmas Trees
Marscapone Torte
Prawn Christmas Tree
Baked Brie in Puff Pastry with Sliced Apples
Sesame Scallops
Mushroom Tarragon Pastries
Marinaded Lamb Skewers
Potato Skins with Sour Cream and Cheese

Brandied Mince Pies

♑ ♑ ♑ ♑ ♑ ♑ ♑ ♑ ♑ ♑ ♑ ♑ ♑ ♑ ♑

Capricorn Party Plan

All recipes are given for 30 people and all can be expanded to accomodate your number of guests.

The day before:
Prepare the marascapone torte
Cook the prawns
Make the brie in puff pastry
Make the sesame scallops
Make the mushroom pastries
Marinade the lamb
Make the potato skins
Make the mince pies

Before the party:	Assemble the smoked salmon canapés
	Turn out and garnish the torte
	Assemble the prawn tree
	Skewer the lamb
During the party:	Mix the martinis
	Reheat the brie
	Broil the sesame scallops
	Reheat the mushroom pastries
	Broil the lamb skewers
	Heat and decorate the potato skins
	Reheat and serve the mince pies

♑♑♑ The Absolutely Perfect Martini ♑♑♑

1 2/3 ounces of dry gin to 1/3 ounce dry vermouth

Chill martini pitcher and 3 ounce cocktail glasses to the point of frost. Fill the pitcher with cracked ice. Measure out the exact ingredients for the number of drinks required, pouring the dry gin first. The gin should "smoke" as it settles over the ice. Add dry vermouth, then stir briskly, strain out ice and pour. Serve with an olive.

1 - 1 1/2 lbs smoked salmon
2 loaves sliced bread, lightly toasted
12 oz soft cream cheese
Juice of 1/2 lemon
Small bowl of canned consommé
Red or black caviar
Sprigs of fresh dill

Cut the toasted bread into small neat triangles, and cut the salmon into the same shapes. Process the little pieces of salmon with the cream cheese and lemon juice. Spread this onto the toast and arrange the salmon on top. Brush with the consommé and then place sprigs of dill on top to resemble Christmas trees. With the tip of a pointed knife, very carefully dot the caviar at the end of the "branches" to look like Christmas ornaments. Arrange on a platter garnished with dill sprigs and lemon slices.

ꕔꕔꕔ Marscapone Torte ꕔꕔꕔ

2 lbs marscapone cheese
1/2 lb cream cheese
Sprinkling of salt and white pepper to taste

1 cup sun dried tomatoes soaked in boiling water for 10
   minutes
2 T olive oil
Black pepper and a little garlic to season

1 cup fresh basil leaves
1/2 cup parsley sprigs to maintain the green color
2 T olive oil
Salt and black pepper to taste

Line a small loaf-shaped pan with cheesecloth or linen. In a cuisinart, mix the cheeses and seasoning lightly until smooth.

Drain the sun-dried tomatoes and chop in the cuisinart with the oil, garlic and pepper.

Chop the basil and parsley with the oil and seasonings.

Layer the torte carefully, smoothing out each layer with a rubber spatula. Start and end with the cheese. Cover tightly with wrap and refrigerate overnight before turning out. Serve on a platter surrounded by Belgian endive leaves, crackers and French bread.

♑♑♑ *Christmas Prawn Tree* ♑♑♑

60 jumbo prawns (or as many as your budget will allow)
4 T olive oil
1/2 cup chopped cilantro
Juice of 3 limes
1 cup white wine
Salt and pepper

Assorted durable greens (not lettuce)
Cocktail sauce

Peel and devein the prawns, and sauté them in olive oil. When just turning pink, add the cilantro, lime juice, wine and seasonings and simmer gently until cooked through, about 3 minutes. Refrigerate well.

Cover a styrofoam cone with the greens using toothpicks. Then toothpick in the prawns in a spiral over the "tree." Serve cold with cocktail sauce.

⑬⑬⑬ Baked Brie in Puff Pastry ⑬⑬⑬

    1 whole wheel of brie cheese
    1 1/2 lbs puff pastry
    1 egg beaten with a pinch of salt
    Red and green apples

Chill the cheese well. Roll out the pastry and cut into two circles, one approximately the diameter of the cheese and the other about 4" larger. Lay the cheese on the larger circle and wet the edges of the pastry. Stick the other circle on top, completely wrapping the cheese, and crimp the edges together. Use pieces of puff pastry to create a design and stick it to the top with water. Brush the top with the egg wash and bake at 400° for about 25 minutes, until golden brown. Serve warm with alternating slices of red and green apples, French bread or crackers. If preparing ahead, reheat the cheese in a conventional or microwave oven until warm.

⑬⑬⑬ Sesame Scallops ⑬⑬⑬

    2 lbs scallops
    1 cup wine, flavored with bay leaf, salt and pepper
    2 lb thin sliced lean bacon
    Sesame seeds

Poach the scallops gently in the wine until just opaque and chill. Cut the bacon into 3" lengths and fry gently to release some of the fat. Wrap the bacon around the scallops, hold with a wooden toothpick and dip into a bowl of sesame seeds. Place onto a cookie sheet until ready for serving. Broil until browned all over.

♑♑♑ *Mushroom Tarragon Pastries* ♑♑♑

8 oz cream cheese
8 oz butter
4 T cream
2 1/2 cups flour
Pinch of salt

4 finely chopped shallots
2 oz butter
1 1/2 lbs mushrooms, cleaned and chopped
Salt and pepper
2 T chopped fresh tarragon
3 eggs
1 cup sour cream

Prepare the pastry: cream the cheese and butter together until smooth, then blend in the cream, seasoning and flour until it forms a dough. Adjust the flour if necessary to make the pastry soft but not sticky. Chill before rolling out.

Saute the shallots and mushrooms in butter and add seasonings. Off the heat, stir in the eggs and sour cream.

Roll out the pastry and, using a fluted cutter, cut out rounds to fit a 1 1/2" muffin pan. Grease the pan, line the cups with the pastry and spoon in the mushroom filling. Bake at 375° for about 15 minutes, until set and golden brown. Top with a sprig of tarragon and serve hot. These pastries can be frozen and reheated later, in an oven or microwave.

ВВВ Marinaded Lamb Skewers ВВВ

3 lbs boned out lamb, from the leg
2 T cumin
Freshly ground black pepper and crushed garlic to taste
2 T ground ginger
2 cups plain yogurt
1 lb Japanese or Chinese eggplant
2 large red onions

Remove any fat from the meat and cut it into neat 1" cubes. Mix the seasonings into the yogurt and marinade the lamb in the mixture overnight. Cut the eggplant into slices, and the onions into chunks. Skewer the meat and vegetables and broil or barbeque for about 10 minutes until cooked through.

ВВВ Potato Skins with Cheese and Sour Cream ВВВ

60 small red creamer potatoes (about 1" across)
Melted butter and salt
1 lb cheddar cheese
1 cup sour cream

Using a melon baller, scoop out the insides of the potatoes. Brush them very lightly with melted butter and sprinkle with salt. Roast at about 375° for about 30 minutes, until turning crisp. Remove from the oven, place a small cube of cheese into each potato and cover until serving time.

Reheat the potatoes until the cheese starts to melt, and pipe a small rosette of sour cream on top.

♑♑♑ Brandied Mince Pies ♑♑♑

2 cups flour
Pinch salt and 1 t cinnamon
4 oz butter
2 oz lard or shortening
1 egg
Cold water to mix
2 lbs mincemeat
About 1 cup brandy

Rub the butter and shortening into the flour, cinnamon and salt until crumbly. Blend in the egg and just enough water to make a soft dough. Roll out thinly. Using a fluted cookie cutter, cut into 2" rounds and line into small muffin pans. Mix some of the brandy into the mincemeat and line this into the pastry. Top with smaller pastry rounds, seal the edges with water and brush the tops with a little milk and sugar. Bake at 400° until golden brown, about 15 minutes.

Serve hot if possible, and just before serving, using a food hypodermic, inject extra brandy into each pie.

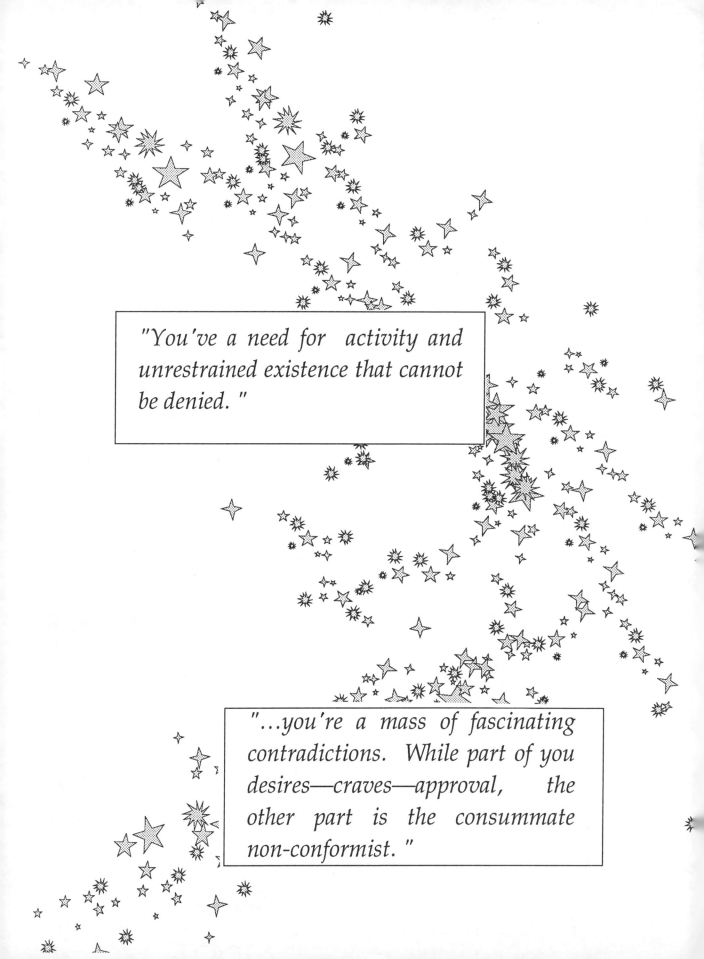

"You've a need for activity and unrestrained existence that cannot be denied."

"...you're a mass of fascinating contradictions. While part of you desires—craves—approval, the other part is the consummate non-conformist."

AQUARIUS
A Progressive Dinner Party
for 12

Bloody Marys
Cheese Fondue with Bread and Fruit

Curried Chicken with Coconut
Almond and Raisin Rice
Cucumber Raita
Peach Chutney
Assorted Sambals: Nuts, Coconut, Raisins, Pickles,
Relishes

Champagne Sorbet
Chocolate Truffles

AQUARIUS

January 20-February 18

Could anyone be both logical *and* intuitive? Eccentric *and* dogmatic? Traditional *and* futuristic? Not likely—unless that "anyone" is you, Aquari.

With two planetary rulers as divergent as Saturn and Uranus pressing your buttons, it's really no wonder that you're a mass of fascinating contradictions. While part of you desires—craves—approval, the other part is the consummate non-conformist.

No matter how conservative the exterior, there's always a "shocking" secret or two tucked away in the closet. (The Sunday School teacher who believes in family nudity, the mathematician who looks for UFOs.)

Actually the whole idea of choice fascinates you. Ideologically at least, you're highly experimental. Surely the concept of alternative lifestyles must have been invented by an Aquari.

"You do your thing and I'll do mine," the motto of the Big Sur crowd back in the 60s, is not only a hallmark of the human potential movement but a personal tenet that you take very seriously. You've a need for activity and unrestrained existence that cannot be denied. To love you is to let you be and in so doing glimpse the New Age challenges ahead.

Though not outwardly aggressive about your ideas—in the fire sign sense of say a Leo or Aries—you retain your calm confidence, clearly, coolly focused on doing your own thing.

Abraham Lincoln and Franklin Roosevelt are classic examples of Aquarius in action. Extremely controversial presidents championing highly unpopular concepts, both stood virtually alone, yet each was able to enact sweeping reforms over bitter opposition.

Unfettered by illusions of the past, the sign of the water bearer trusts in the moment, foreseeing and often creating a more civilized future. The Age of Aquarius is upon us. What better guide than this potential avatar of a new consciousness?

Take Minerva's word for it: what Aquari thinks today is a road map to tomorrow.

air sign

AQUARIUS' Progressive Dinner

It's safe to say that Aquarius is the sign most difficult for others to "read." People with the most random knowledge of astrology can give you a pretty fair description of a Leo or Virgo type and many *think* they know all about Scorpios.

But Aquarius—that's something else again. The only thing everyone agrees upon is that Aquarians are "different." Those born under the sign of the waterbearer are sometimes thought by others to be a little strange. One reason for the confusion is that one Aquari is very unlike another—or like anyone else for that matter. These are the arch kooks of the cosmos.

A bored Aquari with time on her/his hands might very well: rewire

all the lighting in the house, get involved in a charity drive, take a course in a astrology—or astrophysics, go into group therapy, plan a block party, take flying lessons, buy a CB radio and network, design some avant garde clothes, or start a revolution.

All of the above are "typical" Aquarius pursuits. Obviously no one is ever bored around one. Maybe this is why they have so many friends. Consider President Franklin D. Roosevelt and his famous fireside chats. "My friends. . . . ." The magic of this truly Aquarian voice floating out over the air waves encompassed the entire country in a sense of camaraderie and friendship that was almost mystical.

The glyph for the sign, ≋ , symbolizes the water's surface whipped into waves by the wind. This metaphor is intrinsic to Aquarius, a sign that rules both air waves and electrical waves. This is the sign that's linked with all telecommunications —including telepathic. This is also the sign that likes to make waves.

Aquarians consciously create their own reality and since this invariably involves a sense of group destiny—a belief in the good of a common cause—what could be more appropriate than a progressive dinner?

Aquaris are natural stars in group situations where they can balance leadership with fellowship, giving friends lots of space and expecting the same in return. The Aquarian ideals of self actualization and group sharing come readily to the fore in this egalitarian gala which is truly ongoing, forward thinking and even a tad revolutionary.

Sudden flashes of insight and intuition, visions, telepathy or prophetic dreams concerning the future—particularly the future of society—are common to Aquarians. It would be quite natural for three of them to form a common vision and in so doing band together to share their birthday with a wide variety of friends.

What can one expect?   "Merely" the unexpected.

The menu is certain to have a kind of cosmic, "one world" feeling about it. Along with scintillating surprises, there–will–be–that–sudden Aquarian coolness offering piquant contrast and a touch of unexpected elegance.

The decor will be "modern," functional yes, but invariably offbeat with a touch of unexpected humor. The conversation is certain to be outrageous. Though cool and slightly detached in their representation, Aquaris enjoy being shocking. They've a need to defy public opinion. Perhaps they're in this world primarily to shake us up!

At any rate, friends and lovers will have to stay on their toes for new ideas will be the stock and trade.

Just consider some of these revolutionary Aquarians of the past: Susan B. Anthony, Lord Byron, Ayn Rand, Jules Verne, W.C. Fields, Lewis Carroll, Thomas Paine, James Joyce, Gertrude Stein. Or more contemporarily: John Belushi, James Dean, Helen Gurley Brown, Yoko Ono, Norman Mailer, Vanessa Redgrave, Shelley Berman.

Soon, it seems, the unconventional becomes almost normal.

AQUARIUS — A Progressive Dinner for 12

≈ ≈ ≈ ≈ ≈ ≈ ≈ ≈ ≈ ≈ ≈ ≈ ≈

Bloody Marys
Cheese Fondue with Bread and Fruit

Curried Chicken with Coconut
Almond and Raisin Rice
Cucumber Raita
Peach Chutney
Assorted Sambals: Nuts, Coconut, Raisins, Pickles, Relishes

Champagne Sorbet
Chocolate Truffles

≈ ≈ ≈ ≈ ≈ ≈ ≈ ≈ ≈ ≈ ≈ ≈ ≈

Aquarius Party Plan

THE FIRST HOUSE
Before the party: Make fondue and cut up fruit and bread

During the party: Mix the Bloody Marys

THE SECOND HOUSE
The day before: Make curried chicken
                            Make peach chutney

Before the party: Cook rice and store ready to reheat
                            Mix cucumber raita
                            Arrange the sambals

During the party: Reheat curry and rice

THE THIRD HOUSE
The day before: Make sorbet
                            Make the truffles

≈≈≈≈ *Bloody Marys* ≈≈≈≈

Either in individual glasses, or in a pitcher, mix vodka with spicy Bloody Mary mix, and squeeze in fresh lime juice to taste. Serve over ice, with a lime wedge and a trimmed celery stick.

≈≈≈≈ *Cheese Fondue* ≈≈≈≈

2 cloves garlic
2 1/2 cups dry white wine
3/4 lb imported Swiss cheese (Emmenthaler)
3/4 lb Gruyère cheese
2 T cornstarch
1 T dry mustard
1 T paprika
1/4 cup kirsch

Cut the garlic cloves in half and rub the fondue pot with the cut sides. Crush the rest and add to the pot with the wine, and heat gently. Grate the cheeses and combine them with the cornstarch and mustard. Whisk the cheeses slowly into the wine, allowing each handful to melt. Turn the heat down as the mixture thickens. Stir in kirsch and paprika, and taste for seasoning, adding salt, pepper or nutmeg if needed. Cut up French bread, leaving some crust on each piece, and cut fruit and vegetables, e.g., apples, pear, cauliflower, zucchini, jicama into chunks to accompany the fondue.

≈≈≈ *Curried Chicken with Coconut* ≈≈≈

Two 4 lb roasting chickens

Mustard oil or ghee for frying

2 onions, chopped

2 cups chopped celery

2 T curry powder

2 t ground ginger

2 t ground coriander

2 t ground cumin

1 t turmeric

1 t fenugreek (optional)

3 T flour

4-5 cups chicken stock (could be made from the giblets)

4 cloves crushed garlic

3/4 cup finely shredded unsweetened coconut

2 cups boiling water

3 T redcurrant jelly

Juice of 1-2 lemons

1/4 cup cream

Cornstarch to thicken if necessary

Suggested garnishes:

2 cups sliced peaches or mangos

Yogurt topping sprinkled with toasted coconut

Cut the chicken into pieces and brown in hot oil. Use a large frying pan, and do this in several batches without overcrowding the pan. Remove the chicken and then fry the onions and celery for a few minutes. Add these to the chicken and then, using a little more oil as necessary, cook the spices for a few minutes, then add garlic and flour, and blend in the stock. Meanwhile, steep the coconut in the boiling water. Add this nut milk and all ingredients so far to a large pan and cook over gentle heat or in a 350° oven until the chicken is tender.

Finish the sauce with redcurrant jelly, lemon and cream and thicken if needed. Allow to sit overnight, and before reheating remove any excess fat that has risen to the surface. Adjust the curry seasoning to your taste.

Reheat thoroughly on the stove or in a microwave oven and top with the chosen garnish.

≈≈≈ *Almond and Raisin Rice* ≈≈≈

> 3 cups rice of your choice
> Chicken stock for cooking the rice
> 1 t turmeric
> 3-4 T oil or butter
> 3/4 cup chopped green onions
> 1/2 inch chopped ginger root
> 1 cup slivered almonds
> 1/2 cup raisins
> Salt and pepper to taste

Cook the rice according to instructions, using chicken stock instead of water. For an unusual presentation, cook it in 2 separate pans, adding turmeric to one, which will color the rice bright yellow. Drain. Fry the onions, ginger and almonds in butter and then add the raisins and seasoning. Add the rice, or divide in two and add the yellow rice to one half and the white rice to the other. If not needed immediately, turn into a covered buttered pan to reheat in a regular or microwave oven.

≈≈ ≈≈ ≈≈   *Cucumber Raita*   ≈≈ ≈≈ ≈≈

2 European cucumbers
1 t salt
2 cups plain yogurt
1 chopped green chili
Salt and pepper
1 t ground cumin
1 t ground ginger

Peel the cucumbers and grate them coarsely. Sprinkle with salt and drain off the liquid after a while. Mix with the remaining ingredients and chill well to serve as a refreshing accompaniment to the curry.

≈≈ ≈≈ ≈≈   *Peach Chutney*   ≈≈ ≈≈ ≈≈

1 large can sliced peaches or 4-5 fresh peaches
1 1/2 cups brown sugar
1 1/2 cups vinegar
2 onions, finely sliced
3 tomatoes, finely sliced
1 cup currants
1/4 cup crystallized ginger sliced thinly or
1/4 cup ginger marmalade
1 t each allspice and cayenne pepper
2 crushed cloves garlic

If using canned peaches, add all ingredients except the peaches to the syrup in the can and bring to a boil. If using fresh peaches, bring all the ingredients to a boil, adding a cup of water. Peel and slice the fruit. Simmer the mixture gently for about an hour, when the chutney should have thickened. Add the peaches, cook for a few minutes and then chill. If it is to be kept for any length of time, bottle in jars. Serve cold with the curry.

≈≈≈ *Assorted Sambals* ≈≈≈

In small dishes, arrange an assortment of the following accompaniments to the curry:

> Unsweetened coconut flakes
> Sliced bananas
> Raisins
> Chopped tomatoes
> Chutneys or pickles
> Peanuts
> Poppadoms
> Chopped onions

≈≈≈ *Champagne Sorbet* ≈≈≈

If you are short of time, use prepared sherbet or ice cream, but for the more ambitious —

> 2 bottles sweet champagne (it can be inexpensive),
>   well chilled
> 3/4 cup sugar
> 3/4 cup water
> 1/4 cup maple syrup
> 2 packages gelatine
> 3-4 T water or champagne
> Juice of 2 lemons

Mix the sugar, water and syrup and heat until smooth. Sprinkle the gelatine over the water or champagne in a small pan, and when "sponged," gently heat until smooth. Blend the two together. Turn half of it into a food processor (this can be done with an electric mixer) with half the lemon juice and process for 30 seconds. Add about 2 cups champagne and continue to process for another 30 seconds, and then turn into a cold container. Repeat with the other half and 2 more cups of the champagne. Chill for several hours or overnight in the refrigerator. Pour the mixture into an ice cream maker and churn until it reaches the consistency of sherbet. Place container in the freezer to ripen.

To serve, spoon into champagne flutes, top with the extra champagne and garnish with a fresh mint leaf.

AQUARIUS

≈≈≈ *Chocolate Truffles* ≈≈≈

1 lb good quality bittersweet chocolate
2 T instant coffee, dissolved in 1 T water
4 oz unsalted butter
4 oz unblanched almonds
4 T sugar
1 T or so kahlua or liqueur to taste
2 T cream

Coating:
3-4 oz bittersweet chocolate
Few tablespoons cocoa powder

Start by making the praline powder: heat the almonds and sugar together until carmelized to a dark brown. Pour onto a greased metal cookie sheet, and when cooled, grind to a powder. Over a double boiler, melt the chocolate and coffee and then stir in the butter, praline powder, kahlua and cream. Do not let the mixture get too hot. Chill until the mixture can be rolled, and then make 1" balls. Allow to set firmly. Melt the remaining chocolate and sprinkle the cocoa onto wax paper. Dip the truffles first into the chocolate and then into the cocoa, to make an even coating. Keep cool.

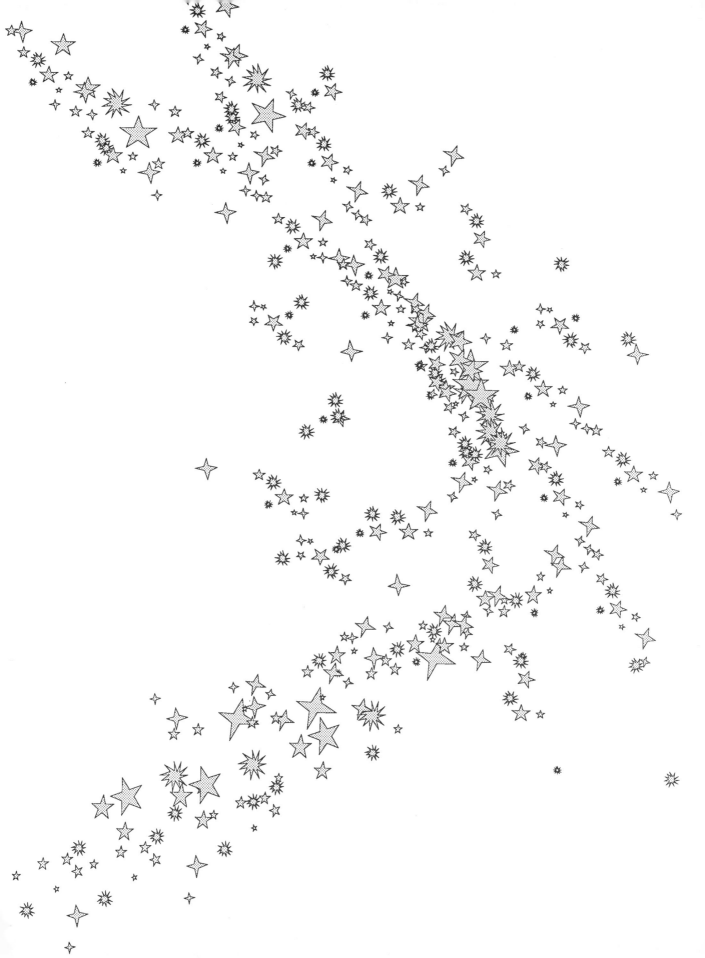

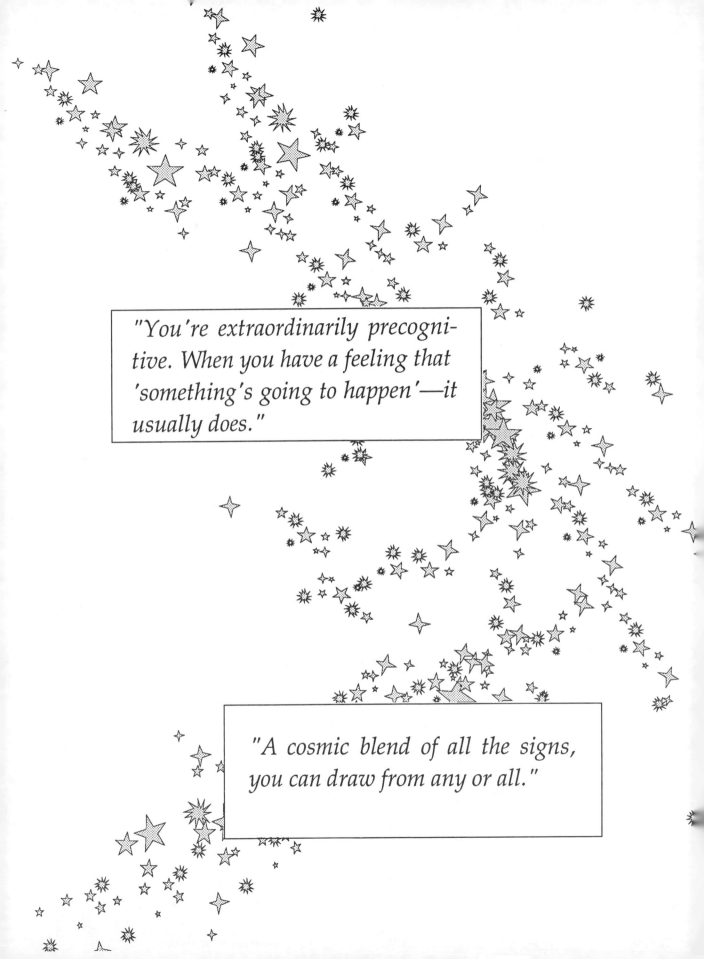

"You're extraordinarily precognitive. When you have a feeling that
'something's going to happen'—it
usually does."

"A cosmic blend of all the signs,
you can draw from any or all."

PISCES
A Come As You Were Party For 20

French 75's

Prosciutto and Melon Boats
Chicken Liver Mousse
Coulibiac with Dill Sauce
Hot Cucumbers
Caponata

Viennese Almond Gateau
Coffee Liqueurs

PISCES

February 19-March 20

You've done it all! At one time or another—in one way or another—you've experienced all the trials and triumphs of life. Seers love to speak of "old souls." Almost always they refer to you. In this life—or possibly in those gone by—you've experienced many existences. Somewhere deep inside, the wisdom remains. You know *all* the answers. The trick is to remember them at the right time.

You can—more than any other sign—see the big picture. For you, all the world's a stage; but the moments of drama are so fleeting, so elusive. Knowing this instinctively, you possess an amazing equanimity to the reversals and upsets of life.

You're also extraordinarily precognitive. When you have a feeling that "something's going to happen"—it usually does. Maybe that's because it's happened before and a part of you remembers, consciously or otherwise; or possibly it's that unique Pisces ability to stand apart from yourself and see yesterday, today and tomorrow as one.

Where Aries is the symbolic baby of the cosmos, often impatient and demanding, you represent eternity. With Aries it's only just begun while you're a compendium of everything that's ever been. A cosmic blend of all the signs, you can draw from any or all.

Of course this means a mixed bag: Virgo's discrimination and organizational skills *as well as* nit picking; lots of Cancer compassion *but* coupled with crabbiness; Scorpio's passion *and* possessiveness you see the problem?

Yet, when you choose to draw on that considerable astral bank account, the possibilities are limitless. The contributions of Pisces are mythic in their magnitude. Consider the ethereal translucence of a Renoir painting, the other worldliness of Rimsky-Korsakov's *Scheherazade.* Nijinsky and Nureyev have defied gravity as surely as Einstein defied physics.

Naturally it never surprises *you* that a simple heart-to-heart chat causes your plants to flourish when others droop; yet Luther Burbank created whole new species through TLC and a little Pisces cajoling.

Need I say it again? A Pisces can do anything and probably has.

water sign

PISCES — A Come As You Were Party

You know the song that goes, "We looked at each other in the same way then, but I can't remember where or when"? It *must* have been written by or for a Pisces.

Other signs get hunches. Scorpio may even do a little witching on the side. But you, Pisces, are the psychic blotter of the Cosmos. Dreamy, poetic, mystical, for you, anything's possible.

If you don't actually embrace the theory of reincarnation with open arms, you're at least considering it. You meet someone new, feel sudden simpatico, and begin to speculate: Did I know you before? Was I Cleopatra and you Mark Anthony? Or were you Josephine to my Napoleon? Do we have a little unfinished business —karmically speaking?

The song offers a clue, "The clothes we were wearing, we were wearing then. . ." What better stimulant to the imagination than a Come as You Were Party?

Since the concept of many lives implies also many loves the combinations could be a colorful scramble. Consider the cast of characters from which to choose: a World War I flying ace chatting with Catherine the Great, Belle Starr with Socrates, George Washington and Jean Harlow.

What better setting for this reunion of potential soulmates than a salon, a salon in the grand tradition of Ninon de Lenclos or George Sand. Sand's great love was Frederic Chopin, a classic Pisces, as was Elizabeth Browning ("How do I love thee, let me count the ways"). Obviously ethereal Pisces has a special enchantment that even rivals Libra in the romance department.

Many psychics believe purple to be the color of the spirit. Variations from lavender to mauve are a natural for your buffet table. For a centerpiece, consider white camellias floating in crystal or a bouquet of violets in a silver compote.

As for the house drink, spirits of a different kind. The French 75 was named for the famous cannon of World I—an indication of its potency.

If this doesn't trigger some past life introspection, nothing will.

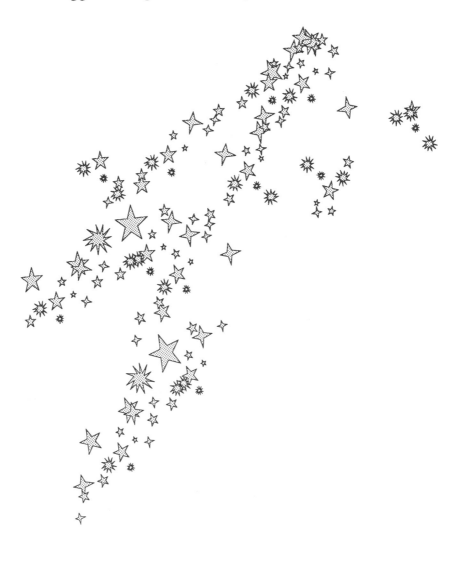

PISCES
A Come As You Were Party for 20

⊬ ⊬ ⊬ ⊬ ⊬ ⊬ ⊬ ⊬ ⊬ ⊬ ⊬ ⊬ ⊬ ⊬ ⊬

French 75's

Prosciutto and melon boats
Chicken liver mousse
Coulibiac with dill sauce
Hot cucumbers
Caponata

Viennese almond gateau
Coffee liqueurs

⊬ ⊬ ⊬ ⊬ ⊬ ⊬ ⊬ ⊬ ⊬ ⊬ ⊬ ⊬ ⊬ ⊬ ⊬

Pisces Party Plan

The day before

Make the chicken liver paté
Make the caponata
Make the gateau

Before the party

Make the melon boat platter
Turn out and garnish the paté
Make the coulibiac and sauce
Prepare the cucumbers
Finish frosting and decorating the gateau
Prepare the coffee and toppings

During the party

Mix the French 75's
Bake the coulibiac
Heat the cucumbers

⓭ ⓭ ⓭ *French 75's* ⓭ ⓭ ⓭

Into each tall glass, place a sugar cube and a squeeze of lemon juice. Add 2 oz of cognac and an ice cube. Fill with iced champagne. Stir and garnish with a lemon slice.

⓭ ⓭ ⓭ *Prosciutto and Melon Boats* ⓭ ⓭ ⓭

3-4 cantaloupes or honeydew melons
1 lb evenly sliced prosciutto or salami
1 lemon or lime

Slice each melon into about 8 slices and peel each one. Using wooden skewers, thread pieaces of prosciutto or salami to resemble the sails of a galleon and attach to the melon "boat." Use small pieces of lemon or lime rind cut into triangular shapes as flags to top the masts. Place the boats on a large platter of crushed ice.

1 can beef consommé

1 package gelatine

4 T sherry or brandy

Sliced black olives, thinly sliced radishes or carrots, chives and herbs for decoration

2 lbs chicken livers

3 finely chopped shallots

1 clove crushed garlic

2 T butter

1/3 cup sherry or brandy

1/2 cup heavy cream

Salt, black pepper

Pinch of allspice and thyme

8 T melted butter

Sprinkle the gelatin into the cold sherry or brandy in a small pan. Without stirring, leave it until it becomes solid or "sponged." Then dissolve it over low heat, and when smooth, gently add the consommé. Cool this aspic and pour a thin layer into a flat mold or terrine, and chill until set. Meanwhile, cut out a decoration of thin vegetable slices, olives and herbs. Dip these in the aspic and place them in a decorative pattern on the bottom of the mold. Chill again, cover with another thin layer of the aspic and chill until firmly set.

Clean the chicken livers, cut them into halves or quarters and sauté them in the butter and garlic until barely cooked, about 5 minutes. Put into the food processor with the cream and seasonings. Add madeira or cognac to the pan and reduce to about 3 T. Scrape into the bowl, blend to a smooth paste and pour in the melted butter. When completely smooth, reseason the mixture if necessary, turn into the prepared mold and chill well until set. For a firmer paté, add a few tablespoons of leftover aspic mixture. Turn out onto a platter to reveal the pattern. Garnish with parsley and olives, and serve with crackers or sliced French bread.

⅓ ⅓ ⅓ *Coulibiac with Dill Sauce* ⅓ ⅓ ⅓

About 1 1/2 lbs puff pastry - homemade or frozen sheets

1 egg beaten with a pinch of salt

Watercress garnish

2 lb fresh salmon

1 cup water or white wine flavored with a bayleaf, onion slice and parsley for poaching

Salt and pepper

Juice of 1/2 lemon

1/4 lb mushrooms

1/2 cup sliced green onions

2 T butter

2 hardboiled eggs

1/2 cup white rice

3 T butter

3T flour

1/2 lb crab meat

1 cup milk

Salt and pepper

1/2 t dill and pinch of mace

Poach the salmon in the flavored water or wine until just cooked, about 10 minutes. Cool, remove the skin and bones and flake the fish. Reduce the poaching liquid to concentrate the flavors and save about 1/2 cup for the sauce. Season the fish with salt, pepper and lemon juice. Saute the onions and sliced mushrooms in butter. Cook and drain the rice. Mix the rice, chopped hardboiled eggs, mushroom mixture and the salmon. In another pan, melt the butter, stir in the flour and whisk in the milk. Heat until the sauce thickens and season to taste, adding the crab.

Roll out two thirds of the puff pastry into an oblong shape, and put half of the salmon mixture onto it in a long strip down the middle. Top this with a layer of crab sauce, then another of salmon mixture and finish with the crab. Roll out most of the remaining pastry and place this on top. Wrap the rest of the pastry around, sealing the edges with water to make a loaf. Turn the loaf over onto a greased baking sheet. Decorate the top with pieces of puff pastry cut into shapes. Brush with beaten egg and bake at 400° until golden brown and puffed, about 30 minutes.

⅓ ⅓ ⅓ *Dill Sauce* ⅓ ⅓ ⅓

4 T butter
4 T flour
1/2 cup poaching liquid
1 cup half and half
Juice of 1 lemon
2-3 T chopped fresh dill
Salt, pepper, and pinch tarragon to taste

Melt the butter, stir in the flour, and whisk in the liquids. Add remaining seasonings and cook gently until the sauce begins to thicken. Serve warm with the coulibiac.

✕ ✕ ✕ *Hot Cucumbers* ✕ ✕ ✕

3 long cucumbers (European type)
1 T salt
2 T vinegar
4 T butter
Salt and pepper to taste
1 T fresh chopped dill
3/4 cup cream (optional)
1/4 cup chopped parsley

Peel the cucumbers, slice them in half lengthwise and neatly scoop out the seeds. Slice into 1/2 " lengths, sprinkle with salt and vinegar and put aside for about 30 minutes. Heat the butter in a large pan and saute the drained cucumber slices on all sides for about 10 minutes, until just tender but still crisp. Season with salt, pepper and dill, and pour over cream and parsley. Serve immediately or chill and reheat later, taking care to keep the cucumbers crisp.

✠ ✠ ✠ *Caponata* ✠ ✠ ✠

3 lb eggplant (Japanese if available)
1 t salt
few T walnut oil as necessary
2 red onions, chopped
3 cloves garlic, crushed
1/2 t ground allspice
1 cup golden raisins
1 cup chopped walnuts
1 lb peeled and diced tomatoes
freshly ground black pepper and salt to taste
1/4 cup balsamic vinegar
grated rind and juice of 1 orange

garnish:
1/2 cup plain yogurt and 1/2 cup Greek olives

Slice and dice the eggplant neatly and sprinkle with salt. Leave to drain for about 30 minutes, and then dry off the liquid with paper towels. Heat a little of the oil in a large pan and saute the onions with the garlic and allspice. Add the eggplant and saute, adding more oil as necessary. Then add the raisins and walnuts and heat through. Finally add the tomatoes, seasonings and orange and cook for about 20 minutes. The caponata should be made ahead to this point to allow the flavors to develop. Serve cold or hot, (it reheats well in a microwave) garnished with yogurt and olives.

✠ ✠ ✠ *Liqueur Coffees* ✠ ✠ ✠

Serve freshly filtered coffee to mix with a variety of appropriate liqueurs, e.g. Bailey's Irish Cream, Grand Marnier, brandy. Serve a mixture of toppings on the side, e.g. whipped cream, cinnamon, grated chocolate, small strips of orange or lemon rind.

⨳ ⨳ ⨳ *Viennese Almond Gateau* ⨳ ⨳ ⨳

8 oz almond paste
Grated rind and juice of 1 lemon
Grated rind of 1 orange
6 egg yolks
1 t vanilla
4 T sugar
6 egg whites
4 additional T sugar
1/2 cup flour
1/2 t baking powder

Beat the almond paste, rinds, juice, yolks, vanilla and sugar until very smooth. In a separate bowl beat the egg whites until stiff but not dry and then beat in the remaining sugar. Fold the meringue lightly into the almond mixture, and then fold in the flour and baking powder. Turn into a greased and floured 10" springform pan and bake at 350° for about 30-35 minutes, until brown on top and firm in the center. Cool completely and split into two layers with a serrated knife.

⨳ ⨳ ⨳ *Frosting and Filling* ⨳ ⨳ ⨳

8 oz cream cheese
3 T sugar
3 T liqueur (kirsch, Amaretto, Cointreau, etc.)
1 cup whipping cream
Garnish: Strawberries and flaked almonds

Whip the cream cheese, sugar and liqueur until smooth, and whi the cream until it holds its shape. Fold together and use as a filling and frosting for the gateau. Garnish and chill until serving time.

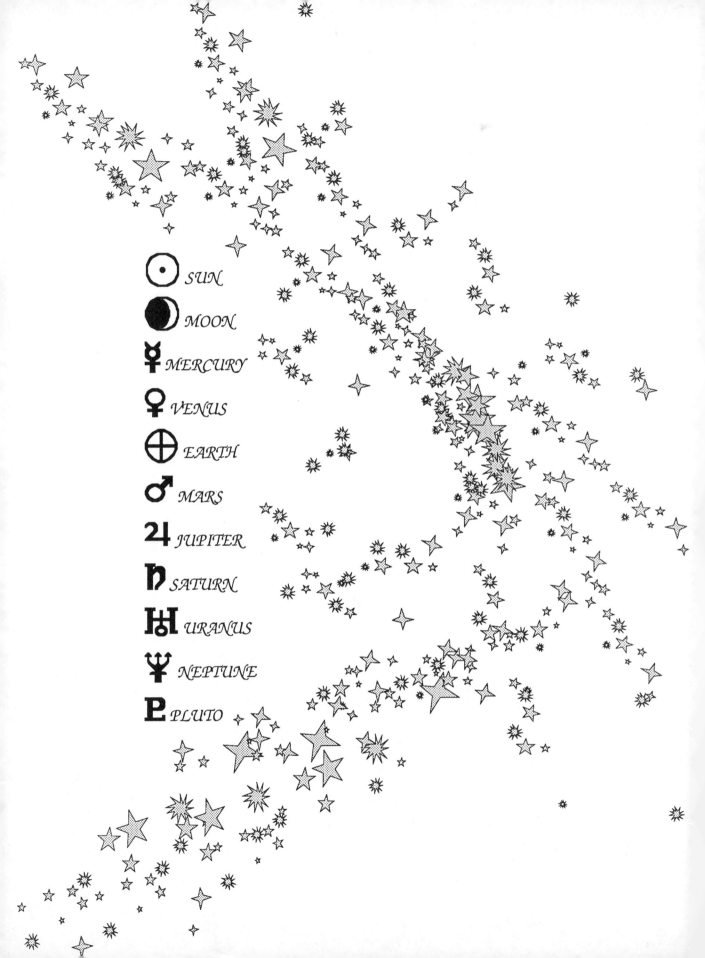

⊙ SUN

☽ MOON

☿ MERCURY

♀ VENUS

⊕ EARTH

♂ MARS

♃ JUPITER

♄ SATURN

♅ URANUS

♆ NEPTUNE

♇ PLUTO

Minerva's Moon Notes ◑

Have you ever met someone born on your birthday? And then wondered about the *differences* in your personalities? Seemingly you should be twins—on the inside at least. But why, you've wondered, does he or she come on so strong, when your style is much more low-keyed.

The first and most important reason for those differences has to do with something called the ascendant or rising sign. While the sun sign determines the inner personality—something we don't always want others to see—the ascendant indicates the style of its manifestation. It has a lot to do with how we *allow* others to see us. Some say the ascendant is where the camera clicked when you were born. It represents your personality as others initially see it and may be quite different from the person you are inside.

Occasionally it all comes together very easily. If you happen to be born with the ascendant in your sun sign, you'll be what's known as a double (double Aries, double Gemini, double whatever). As a result, your personality will be more integrated than if you had a vastly different ascendant from your sun sign.

However this combination is unusual—since the ascendant changes every two hours—and that's why it's often very difficult for us to guess someone's sign. What you see is rarely what you've got. An ascendant is actually a kind of mask. The airy, gentle diplomacy of a Libra ascendant overlaying the smoldering fires of a Scorpio, for instance. The strength of an ascendant may also explain why you sometimes don't feel totally at home with your sun sign. It may truly be that the quiet reasoning effect of your Virgo rising is far stronger than your Leo sun would indicate.

Then, there's another major factor that makes each of us unique and that's our moon sign. Some believe that the position of the moon reveals karma—who or what we were in a past life or at the very least ancestral memories. For certain it has a great deal to do with our dreams, the person we would like to be. Here's how it works:

🌑 **Moon in Aries**—Whatever's going on in your life, you'd like to be a mover and a shaker. You're impatient and want to go! You get revved up about a lot of issues. Men with Aries moons find themselves attracted to independent, go-getter type women.

🌑 **Moon in Taurus**—Whether you are or not you'd like to be rich and comfortable and give a lot of careful thought and concentration to the acquisition of the good things in life.

🌑 **Moon in Gemini**— You'd like to write or at least communicate in some highly meaningful way. A man with this placement will invariably find himself drawn to a woman involved in communications. Mental stimulation is imperative to you and one way or another you'll have it.

🌑 **Moon in Cancer**—This placement is very strong, possibly stronger than your sun sign. You're a very caring person and very psychic too—you *know* that. You're lucky too in that you've been granted a cosmic boon, a sense of feeling free to be exactly who and what you are.

🌑 **Moon in Leo**—Whatever your outward demeanor, somewhere inside you long to be a star. And given your optimism and youthful manner, chances are that you will shine for you're nothing if not a people person. The challenge here is to rise above egotism, possibly a vestige of another time.

🌑 **Moon in Virgo**—You're instinctively conscientious because you just naturally want to do a good job. You're instinctively psychic too and analytical. Are you also instinctively nit picking? Try to rise above it.

🌑 **Moon in Libra**— Making the right choice is so natural that you'd be a marvelous judge or decorator. Harmony in life is a primary objective—particularly where relationships are concerned. A man with this placement will seek out beautiful, seemingly childlike women.

🌑 **Moon in Scorpio**—Look out world! However placid your exterior may seem, inside you're a smoldering volcano waiting to erupt. You have challenges—*you* know what they are—to overcome. Could be a little karmic bookkeeping.

🌑 **Moon in Sagittarius**—Though you may spend a lot of time speculating on the nature of reality, it doesn't prevent you from having a good time. Life is a cabaret, you say. Try not to make too many promises—even you can't do it all.

🌑 **Moon in Capricorn**—Secret desires for power and glory are hard to deny. Your challenge is to rise above being a workaholic. Consider the AA prayer: God give me the strength to change what I can, accept what I can't and know the difference.

🌑 **Moon in Aquarius**—Are you a closet astrologer? You're certain to be innovative, humanitarian, a "New Age" thinker. Whatever your outward demeanor, "Don't fence me in" is a private theme. If a man, you'll be drawn to highly intelligent, independent women.

🌑 **Moon in Pisces**—The psychic blotter of the cosmos, a kind of Peter Pan type who may never grow up, you've a great sense of humor; but simply must learn to assert yourself!

How to penetrate these inner secrets? It's simple. An inexpensive computerized chart—many are available for as low as $5—will reveal all. The purpose behind getting this additional information is to broaden your party repertoire. A moon party honoring your secret side or that of a lover would be fun. Or what about an ascendant soiree—the consummate masquerade. The possibilities are absolutely cosmic!

ABOUT THE AUTHORS

Minerva

Minerva's popular column, *Horoscope*, appears weekly in the *San Francisco Chronicle*. Turning to page 16 of the *Chronicle's Sunday Date Book* has become a ritual for readers all over the Bay Area. Minerva also writes on astrological subjects for magazines.

Jane Hammond

London born, Jane Hammond was graduated from the University of Durham, after which she worked for three years at Oxford University in Physics and Physical Chemistry.

Upon moving to California in 1975, she started a cooking school specializing in French cooking, party giving and pastry workshops.

Subsequently she launched *Jane Hammond Events, Inc.*, a catering business with headquarters in Berkeley and kitchen in San Francisco.

Jane and her husband John, a San Francisco labor lawyer, live in Berkeley with their two children.

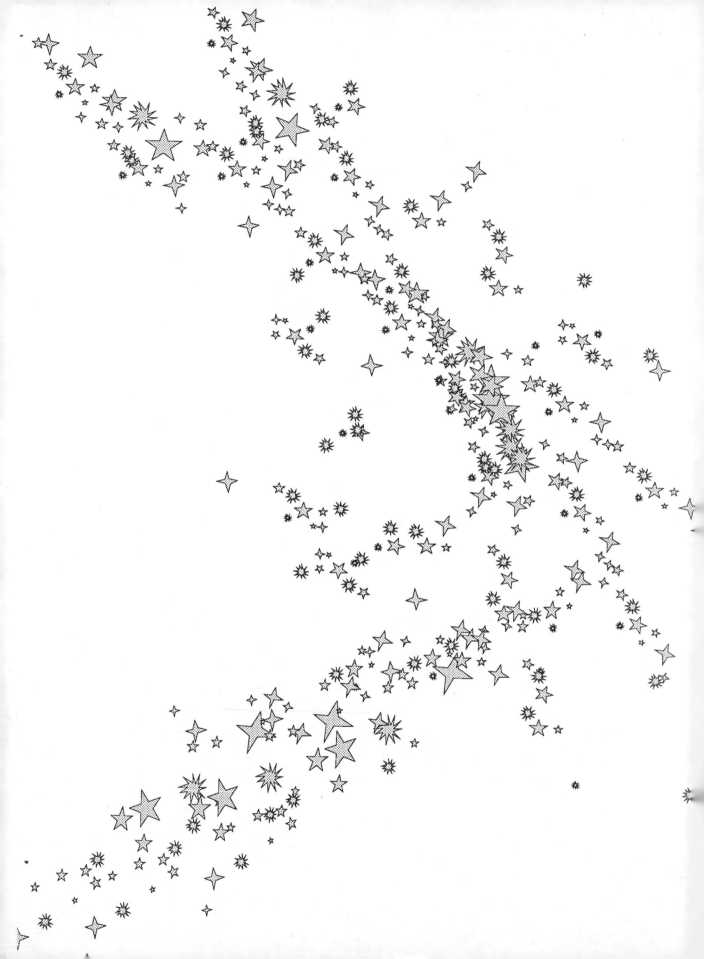